Legends *of* Animation

William
Hanna & Joseph
Barbera

Legends of Animation

Tex Avery:
Hollywood's Master of Screwball Cartoons

Walt Disney:
The Mouse that Roared

Matt Groening:
From Spitballs to Springfield

William Hanna and Joseph Barbera:
The Sultans of Saturday Morning

Legends *of* Animation

William
Hanna & Joseph
Barbera

The Sultans of Saturday Morning

Jeff Lenburg

CHELSEA HOUSE
An Infobase Learning Company

Clifton Park - Halfmoon Public Library
475 Moe Road
Clifton Park, New York 12065

William Hanna and Joseph Barbera: The Sultans of Saturday Morning

Chelsea House
An Infobase Learning Company
132 West 31st Street
New York NY 10001

Library of Congress Cataloging-in-Publication Data
Lenburg, Jeff.
  William Hanna and Joseph Barbera : the sultans of Saturday morning/Jeff Lenburg.
— 1st ed.
    p. cm. — (Legends of animation)
  Includes bibliographical references and index.
  ISBN-13: 978-1-60413-837-5 (hardcover : alk. paper)
  ISBN-10: 1-60413-837-8 (hardcover : alk. paper) 1. Hanna, William, 1910–2001—
Juvenile literature. 2. Barbera, Joseph—Juvenile literature. 3. Animators—United
States—Biography—Juvenile literature. I. Title. II. Title: Sultans of Saturday morning.
III. Series.
  NC1766.U52H36355 2011
  741.5'80922—dc22
  [B]   2010051582

Chelsea House books are available at special discounts when purchased in bulk quantities for businesses, associations, institutions, or sales promotions. Please call our Special Sales Department in New York at (212) 967-8800 or (800) 322-8755.

You can find Chelsea House on the World Wide Web at
http://www.chelseahouse.com

Text design by Kerry Casey
Cover design by Takeshi Takahashi
Composition by EJB Publishing Services
Cover printed by Yurchak Printing, Landisville, Penn.
Book printed and bound by Yurchak Printing, Landisville, Penn.
Date printed: May 2011

Printed in the United States of America
2503
10 9 8 7 6 5 4 3 2 1

This book is printed on acid-free paper.

To my dear friend, spiritual mentor,
and a pretty decent racquetball player,
Carolyn Lygo, for your love, support, and inspiration over the years.

CONTENTS

	Acknowledgments	9
1	The Accidental Artist	11
2	The Incessant Doodler and Dreamer	21
3	Chasing Their Cartoon Dreams	32
4	Fathering Filmdom's Most Famous Cat and Mouse	47
5	Blazing a New Path	73
6	Conquering Prime-time with America's Favorite Prehistoric Family	93
7	Changing the Face of Saturday Morning Television	110
8	New Beginnings	131
	Selected Resources	153
	Selected Bibliography	157
	Index	159
	About the Author	167

ACKNOWLEDGMENTS

First and foremost, my sincere thanks to two legends of animation and friends—the late William Hanna and Joseph Barbera—for sharing their recollections with me originally for my formative chapter on their careers in my book *The Great Cartoon Directors*, the foundation for this book, and for subsequent chats with them without whom this project would not have been possible.

Many thanks to the staffs of the Margaret Herrick Library of the Academy of Motion Picture Arts and Sciences, the Archives of Performing Arts and the Regional History Collections at the University of Southern California, the Los Angeles Times Photographic Archive of the University of California, Los Angeles Public Library, the Museum of Modern Art, and Arizona State University West Fletcher Library for their personal assistance and contributions of additional research necessary for the successful completion of this project.

Also, my profuse gratitude to the following newspapers, trade publications, and journals: *The Guardian* (London), *Hartford Courant*, *Los Angeles Times*, *New York Times*, *Observer* (London), *Washington Post*, *Box Office*, *Hollywood Reporter*, *Film Daily*, *Motion Picture Herald*, *Variety*, *Animation Magazine*, *Film Comment*, *Funnyworld*, *Griffithiana*, and *Mindrot*, for their extensive coverage of noteworthy facts and information, which I found of great value in writing and researching this biography.

Lastly, my thanks to many others personally involved throughout the various stages of this project over the years, namely Hanna-Barbera

Productions, Metro-Goldwyn-Mayer, Turner Entertainment, Cartoon Network, and to my editor, James Chambers, for his unwavering support and enthusiasm throughout.

The Accidental Artist

One of film and television's most prolific and celebrated partnerships, they rocketed to the top after dreaming up a menacing cat and cherubic mouse, known as Tom and Jerry, in 114 outrageous slapstick theatrical cartoons throughout the 1940s and 1950s. Producing roars of laughter and unmitigated critical acclaim, this creative duo earned a record 13 single-series Oscar nominations (and two more for unrelated shorts), winning seven gold statuettes—a feat to which no other animator or director can lay claim. As the largest American producer of animated entertainment and with a studio bearing their names, this eight-time Emmy-winning duo also produced more than 3,000 half-hours of cartoons—some 300 productions in all—including 119 animated series, 87 live-action and animated specials, eight feature films, 18 made-for-television films, and seven direct-to-video movies, featuring the likes of Huckleberry Hound, Yogi Bear, Quick Draw McGraw, The Flintstones, Top Cat, The Jetsons, Space Ghost, Josie and the Pussycats, Scooby-Doo, and countless others, that have entertained generations and left an indelible mark on American pop culture. For their rich legacy of achievements and profound impact on the world, these two milestone makers will never be forgotten. Their names are William Hanna and Joseph Barbera.

11

The businessman of the two, William (Bill) Hanna, was born on July 14, 1910, in Melrose, New Mexico, to his father, William John Hanna, and his mother, Avice Joyce, of Irish decent, whose maiden name was Denby. Her father, T. B. S. Denby, was a circuit judge in the territory of New Mexico. Bill was the third of seven children, including six sisters, Lucille, Connie, Norma, Marion, Evelyn, and Jessilee, and the only son in the family that he once described as "very close," without the usual sibling rivalry. His dad was easygoing and independent; his mother kind and generous and the strict disciplinarian of the two.

Throughout Bill's childhood, William was the sole breadwinner while Avice, a "formidable pioneer and a woman of true grit," as Bill once put it, was a stay-at-home mother who ran the entire household, cooking and cleaning, like many women back then did. As a superintendent for the Thomas Haverty Company, William oversaw the construction and development of water and sewer systems throughout most of the Western United States. Some of Bill's happiest memories growing up were accompanying his father to work and watching him in action. William's work, however, kept him away from home for long periods of time. So the burden of rearing all seven children often fell on Avice, a warm-hearted woman and devout Christian with a firm resolve to raise them, as Bill once stated, as "God-fearing, kindly, industrious people," and who made her children attend church every Sunday.

From the dustbowl of New Mexico, Bill and his family moved to the soggy and lushly forested and grassy meadowlands of Baker City, Oregon, in the upper northern region of the state, when he was three years old. William was assigned to supervise construction of the Balm Creek Dam located in the Whitman National Forest. The family lived in a modest home on 10 sprawling acres that included a chicken house and homegrown crops, such as corn. One of Bill's proudest moments, knowing his dad played a role in the dam's completion, was watching a stream of swarming trout in a stock pond that crewmen created on one side of the dam. "You could literally reach in and grab the fish for your supper," he recalled.

In 1915, when he was five, Bill's family moved a third time, this time to Logan, Utah, where William landed work as a supervisor for construction of a new railroad station in town. That year, Bill entered first grade while his six other sisters were also enrolled in the local school, just a few blocks from their home. Always a curious child, although he rarely caused trouble, Bill's curiosity got the best of him one time in 1917. After eying a bird's nest high up in a tree, he decided to climb the tree to see it up close. He encountered something he did not expect: a huge spider web and a big spider. Panic-stricken, he fell to the ground, breaking his arm in the process.

That same year, the Hanna family was on the move again. Accepting the position of supervisor with the Thomas Haverty Company, William relocated them to California. With young Bill's arm wrapped in a sling, they boarded the train bound for California and made San Pedro their home for the next two years. Like a family whose mother or father served in the military, they never stayed in one place long. They frequently changed residences before renting a cottage on 69th Street in Los Angeles, and later, in 1919, a small house at 9523 Anzac Avenue in Watts, a suburb of Los Angeles.

Bill made friends easily wherever they lived. Such was the case in Watts, where he developed close friendships with three boys his age: G. D. Atkinson, Bill Tweedy, and Jack Ogden. Encouraged by his parents, he joined the Boy Scouts, Troop 2 of the Watts District, with his fellow 12-year-old friends. They enjoyed exciting excursions with other scout members, such as going to the beach, hiking up the Cahuenga Pass, and camping outdoors in the famous Hollywood Hills, while learning many important life-lessons and a fundamental set of principles, including the all-important Boy Scout motto, "Be Prepared."

RESPECTING THE VALUE OF HARD WORK

Throughout his childhood, Bill maintained a close-knit relationship with his father. He continued spending time with him on the job with his crew, working as a water boy, and later as a laborer on different construction sites. One thing that became apparent to Bill was the close bond his father had with his crew, like extended members of his family, and the love and respect they had for him. As Bill later said,

"I grew accustomed from a very young age to finding a job, learning and respecting manual labor, and making my own money."

As a result, Bill appreciated the value of money and hard work, never taking anything for granted. With his dad allowing him the sense of independence few teenagers had in those days, he often went alone to the local theater to catch the latest silent motion picture. For the price of a 10-cents admission, he watched the likes of Charlie Chaplin, Douglas Fairbanks, and Mary Pickford, major screen stars in their day, on the big screen, along with many animated cartoon shorts preceding the main feature.

One of Bill's favorite cartoon characters was Felix the Cat, whose onscreen antics and personality were both funny and Chaplinesque. As he said, it became his "first exposure to what would later popularly become known in the animation industry as 'personality animation'" and "made moviegoing a real event for me."

Thanks to the support and encouragement of their parents, Bill and his sisters followed "our own interests and developed whatever talents we felt God had given us." Creativity ran deep in his family. Avice was a prolific writer. She wrote many beautiful poems and essays, mostly spiritual in nature. Although her work was never published, her literary aspirations rubbed off on two of Bill's sisters. Norma, the youngest, would later publish several essays and articles in various religious publications and enjoy a successful writing career. His aunt also wrote Westerns for radio.

Unlike them, however, Bill had yet to find his creative niche, but the artistic endeavors of his mother and two sisters left a lasting impression on him. He took up the practice of writing his own verses and poems on paper ("whimsical little things about cats and mice, boys and girls, good feelings and hope," he later said). He enjoyed the rhythm and rhyme of writing and kept composing more verses and occasional poems, developing a simultaneous interest in music. During his adolescence, he took both piano and saxophone lessons and later studied piano composition while in high school. Bill also became well versed in drawing. He exhibited his earliest cartoon skills in the school's paper with his fellow classmate Irven Spence, who later became a fellow animator when they both worked at Metro-Goldwyn-Mayer.

Even so, Bill never thought of music or writing as a serious career. Nor did he intend to become an artist. Instead, he favored mathematics and journalism and sports in high school, and did not have a clear idea of what profession he wanted to pursue or what he wanted to do with his life. He knew this much for certain: He did not want to follow in his father's footsteps and become a construction supervisor.

After graduating from Compton High School in 1929, the strapping 18-year-old teen enrolled at Compton Junior College, majoring in journalism. That same year, the Great Depression struck, causing one of the worst economic disasters in America's history. With the country in such peril, Bill was forced to drop out of college and find a job. By this time, William had retired from his job with the Thomas Haverty Company, so nobody in his family was employed. That all changed when C. L. Peck, a contractor who had previously worked with his father, offered his dad a job as a crew supervisor overseeing construction of the Pantages Theater in Hollywood. He accepted and moved them to Hollywood, where they rented a small house, and he also managed to get his son a job with the company working with the structural engineers. The job entailed straddling scaffolds crossing girded steel beams several stories high. Bill did not last long on the job. One day, he stumbled and fell one story and broke his arm and ended up in the hospital. He realized afterward that he had better seek a career in which he used his head instead of doing physical labor.

Six months later, after the palatial art deco–styled Pantages Theatre at Hollywood and Vine was completed, Bill was once again unemployed. Driving around downtown Hollywood in his slick 1925 Ford Coupe that he had bought with money saved from previous jobs, he inquired about work. But, as he once wrote, every day he ran into the same scenario—lots of "Heads shaking, apologies, nothing, nothing, nothing."

One afternoon, a service station operator on Sunset Boulevard, who had spotted Bill making his usual daily rounds for work, approached him when he pulled in and offered him a job washing cars. Grateful for the opportunity, he worked that job for about a week until one evening in 1930, when he met Jack Stevens, a young man who was dating his sister Marion. Stevens worked for a company called Pacific Title & Art Studio, owned by Leon Schlesinger. Schlesinger had under contract two former Disney animators, Hugh Harman and Rudolf Ising, to produce the studio's early *Merrie Melodies* and *Looney Tunes* cartoons for which Schlesinger served as producer. Stevens had heard Harman and Ising were hiring people and he recommended Bill look them up.

Desperate for a better paying job, Bill hopped in his Ford Coupe and maneuvered through heavy traffic to the tiny Harman-Ising Studio, located on the second floor of a white stucco building on Hollywood Boulevard. At this point, he still had not decided on pursuing a career as an artist and the job he sought was another manual labor position: studio janitor.

After entering the studio, Bill was interviewed by Ray Katz, head of personnel. Katz liked him so much that he introduced him to Harman and Ising, who offered him the job. Earning $18 a week, he started the next day. Having developed a strong sense of rhyme from writing occasional poems and verses, Bill felt the names of his new bosses had a nice ring to them, "Harmonizing." He looked at that as a good omen of things to come.

LEARNING HIS CRAFT

Bill did not sweep floors and empty wastebaskets for long. A short time after joining the studio, he was promoted to the entry-level position of cel washer in the ink and paint department, where he washed the ink and paint off acetate cels used to animate cartoons. A few weeks later, he was promoted again to head of the department to supervise a team of seven women. Working his way up the studio ladder, Bill gained a firsthand understanding of the entire process of how cartoons were made—from developing storylines and storyboards, to inking and coloring around 6,000 drawings, to graphically telling the story in a single seven-minute cartoon. Many of the cartoons he worked on were

Bill (right) is pictured with his partner Joe Barbera after their teaming in 1939 to create their famous cat-and-mouse cartoon characters for Metro-Goldwyn-Mayer, Tom and Jerry.

early *Looney Tunes* and *Merrie Melodies* for Warner Bros., starring a little black boy, Bosko, and his girlfriend, Honey. The first 35-millimeter animated cartoon he saw in finished form directed by Ising, using a small projector called a Movieola, was the first Warner Bros. cartoon—and never-released pilot for the *Bosko* series—*Sinkin' in the Bathtub*.

The whole medium of animation and the work that Ising did intrigued Bill to the point where he started staying extra hours after work to spend more time with the pioneer animator. One thing led to another, with him working his day job in the ink and paint department and then at night (until midnight) with Ising, developing material for his latest cartoon. Bill offered him his ideas, suggestions, and gags to use in his cartoons. Soon he was working with both Harman and Ising outside his usual job description, writing whimsical title songs they incorporated into some of their early *Looney Tunes* and *Merrie Melodies*. He also put his knowledge of music and rhythm to good use by assisting Harman with the timing or synchronization of some of the scenes in their productions. As a result, Bill gained a tremendous appreciation besides hands-on experience in all facets of the making of cartoons.

In 1933, his third year with the studio, Bill ran into a little trouble with his bosses. At the time, Ising hired his girlfriend, Irene Hamilton, to work under Bill in the ink and paint department. Her hiring seemed fine until he learned Ising was paying her an unheard of $60 a week, far and above the meager $37.50 they were paying him to do the same job.

Such injustice did not set well with Bill, who drove to Walt Disney Studios to apply for a job as the head of its ink and paint department. Personnel dispatched him to meet with Disney himself. During the course of their interview, he explained his dilemma. The whole time the rail-thin mustachioed animator sat silently as Bill did most of the talking until finally he spoke up. "Well, I'll tell you, Bill," he said, "We already have a girl in our ink and paint department who's doing a hell of a good job. I suggest you go back and tell Rudy about your problem and I'll bet you that you get your money."

Right after his meeting, Disney must have called Ising to tip him off. As soon as Bill returned to Harman-Ising Studios and Ising spotted him, he told him, "Bill, you're going to get your raise. From now on you'll be drawing $60 a week."

Being single and almost 21 years of age, Bill now made more money than he had ever dreamed of. On weekends, he visited his parents and sisters at home, and occasionally dated. Due to his recent raise, he also helped supplement his parents' income and moved them into a much larger apartment than the one he occupied by himself.

By March 1933, that all changed when Leon Schlesinger ended his agreement with Harman-Ising to produce cartoons for him and Warner Bros. He took many of their employees with him to work at his studio on the Warner's lot. Bill was one of the loyal few who stayed behind among a small staff Harman and Ising retained. He survived some very lean times by doing occasional, small animation jobs. This went on until Harman and Ising signed a deal, announced in the *Hollywood Reporter* on January 4, 1934, after animator Ub Iwerks' deal expired, to produce cartoons for Metro-Goldwyn-Mayer (MGM), starting that February.

In recognition of his loyalty, Harman and Ising provided Bill, a more mature 23 years of age, with opportunities to make his own cartoons utilizing his innate writing, animating, and timing skills to direct his own projects. The first cartoon he directed was *To Spring*, a seven-minute short celebrating springtime, which he produced in association with esteemed animator Paul Fennell. Bill was beyond thrilled when he held the finished nitrate film in his hands and his name flickered across the small screen of the Movieola, "Directed by William Hanna."

Harman and Ising had hoped that by giving Bill the chance to direct they would be able to increase the volume of their productions, but such was not the case. They had acquired a reputation in the industry for being slow in delivering the number of cartoons MGM had contracted them to produce. Eventually this would work against them.

In the meantime, Bill's young life was about to change for the better. Mo Caldwell, one of the studio's writers, introduced him to the twin sister of a girl he was dating, Violet Wogatzke. She worked as a secretary for a Los Angeles insurance company, and he suggested they go on a double date. Bill agreed. The moment he set eyes on the petite brown-haired beauty, he was smitten. Violet was three years younger than him, but Bill was captivated by her self-assuredness, intelligence, and independence, and another important thing they had in common: their love of family.

On August 7, 1936, after a year-long courtship, they were married in a simple ceremony at Immaculate Conception Church. The reception was held at a restaurant on Hollywood Boulevard before they embarked on a two-week honeymoon to San Francisco and Lake Tahoe.

From the beginning and throughout their married life, Violet doted on Bill and was supportive of Bill's career in animation. After their honeymoon, Bill decided to pursue opportunities to direct his own cartoons in earnest. He spoke to Harman and Ising of his pent-up desire to helm more films. Both were willing to give him more opportunities to direct and even produce his own cartoons as part of meeting their contractual obligations with MGM.

As it turned out, MGM had other plans. The studio canceled its contract with Harman and Ising in late 1937. Citing significant cost overruns and Harman-Ising's inability to produce "an adequate supply of cartoons" under their terms of their studio contract, they stopped distribution of their Harman-Ising cartoons by that December. The news of their termination signaled to Bill the end of his chances to direct and, more importantly, to continue his association with two colleagues whom he admired and respected.

With the threat of major layoffs looming, Bill was given a reprieve. Fred Quimby, now the head of MGM's newly forming cartoon department, called him that month. Impressed by his directorial work on *To Spring*, he offered him a job to head his own cartoon unit as a director and story editor. Delighted by his sudden good fortune, Bill and Violet moved and rented a small one-bedroom apartment closer to the studio in Culver City. Thus, the most important chapter of his young career was about to commence.

The Incessant Doodler and Dreamer

Meanwhile, clear across the country on the East Coast, a natural doodler and dreamer, one of nine Sicilian children, was born at 10 Delancey Street in the heart of New York's Little Italy quarter on the Lower East Side. He was a good-looking, smiling, dark-curly haired kid by the name of Joseph Barbera.

Brought into this world on March 24, 1911, Joe was the third and youngest son of immigrant parents, Vincent Barbera and Francesca Calvacca, after two older brothers, Larry and Ted. Each were raised in a traditional Italian-speaking household by their mother, married at age 16, and their grandmother on their mother's side, also named Francesca, who helped rear all nine children, including her own five sons, after emigrating to New York City from the southern coast of Sicily in 1898. Among his family members, Joe was the only one who could draw.

When Joe was four months old, Vincent moved the family to Flatbush, Brooklyn, a neighborhood of tree-lined streets and parkways, which, as Joe wrote in his autobiography, "was a step up for an immigrant family in those days." Those who lived on his block were hardworking and did not take handouts. Instead, they were willing to work any job they could with a great determination to succeed.

Joe's father was creative with his hands. By trade, Vincent was a barber who cut both men's and women's hair. One of his specialties was the "Marcel wave" that created deep, regular waves in the customer's hair with a regular curling iron. By the time he was 25, his business blossomed. He owned three shops in Brooklyn on Church Avenue, Newkirk Avenue, and Cortelyou Road that flourished. As a result of his father's success, Joe and his brothers grew up comfortably. But the downside of Vincent's burgeoning business was, despite the huge financial payoff, his family saw less and less of him as he tended to the business of operating his shops. His frequent absences also involved squandering his fortune on gambling on horses at the Aqueduct and Belmont horse tracks, where he took Joe for the first time in 1916 when he was only five years old.

Over a period of time, Joe hardly saw Vincent. He would show up every so often and simply toss a wad of money, as much as $2,000 to $3,000, on the table, for his mother to live on. The high-living, fancily dressed Vincent tried his hand at investing in real estate, buying an apartment building to rent out and then selling it for a quick profit. A man who liked living in the fast lane, he was restless and impatient, breaking out in violent rages and terrorizing the family by mostly "yelling, gesturing, and stamping about the parlor barber shops," as Joe recalled. Joe's mother was often exasperated by his fits of rage that accelerated to him actually threatening her. During such episodes, young Joe took refuge under his bed. Grabbing the springs underneath the box spring, he suspended himself off the floor as Vincent stormed through the room, fuming and flogging the furniture and floor with his black leather belt.

Then, one day, Vincent stopped coming around and disappeared. Occasionally, Joe reached out and made contact. He would call one of his barber shops to get a free haircut, but such occasions were without the close bond typical between a father and son. By the time Joe began attending Erasmus Hall High School in Brooklyn, the contact between them lessened until eventually he lost touch with Vincent altogether. By then his maternal uncle Jim, one of his mother's brothers, became the father figure he had never had. He was, as Joe once wrote, "kind, generous and . . . wonderful." For one week each summer, he took Joe with his wife, Joe's Aunt Tess, to the Catskills to board with another couple for $10.

In 1926, at age 15, Joe and his family moved to live with his grandmother and grandfather in their small two-family house in Flatbush. Thereafter, they moved frequently, living a nomadic existence.

When his still-married parents enrolled him in his first grade at Holy Innocents, a Catholic elementary school in the heart of Brooklyn, Joe discovered his ability to draw. His apparent talent impressed the nuns so much they "put me to work," as he described it They would plant the youngster in front of the blackboard and have him draw illustrations from the Bible, including one of Jesus entering Jerusalem surrounded by "palms and people waving." He became so popular in the class that the nuns frequently used him to do more drawings from the Bible and even brought visitors into the classroom to watch him in action.

Unfortunately, the way his first-grade class was structured, he never had to study or do homework, and his mother noticed every time he came home covered in chalk dust. As Joe once wrote, " . . . I was learning absolutely nothing. Reading I had picked up on my own, but I couldn't add, subtract, divide, or multiply." Outraged by his lack of progress, Francesca pulled him out of Holy Innocents and entered him into public school, PS 139, where he excelled in something other than drawing: sports, where he became a championship high jumper.

TAPPING INTO HIS FIRST LOVE: DRAWING

In 1924, as a robust 13-year-old freshman at Erasmus Hall High, located between Flatbush, Bedford, Church, and Snyder Avenues and added to the National Register of Historic Places in 1975, Joe rediscovered his love of drawing. It happened while sitting across from a pretty blond classmate in music class, Stephanie Bates. Inspired by her beauty, the street-wise Italian charmer began sketching her and gave the sketches to her after class and, seizing the moment, asked her to the movies.

During Joe's time at Erasmus Hall High, the school underwent the construction of a quadrangle of buildings surrounding the existing structures to accommodate the booming population, Joe made good with his art. He entered some of his work in art contests and won and became the editor of the school newspaper, *The Dutchman*, contributing numerous original cartoons that were published. Despite his tremendous knack for drawing, he later admitted he was less interested in art than he was in literature. He enjoyed writing in English class and so impressed his teacher with an essay he wrote about Cossacks attacking a village that she asked him to read it aloud to the entire class. When it came to literature, action-adventure stories were his favorite genre growing up—one reason many years later after cofounding Hanna-Barbera studios he was always attracted to them. Often, he stayed up past his bedtime reading stories with a flashlight under the covers until Vincent would burst into his room and snatch them from his hands.

Joe's all-time favorite was *The Book of Knowledge*. He sat riveted, reading about the myths, legends, and tales of great heroic acts, including the Crusades adventure steeped in magnificent chivalry, *Chason de Roland*, the story of the dashing medieval hero Roland. (The same name he later chose as his middle name for his Confirmation.)

During high school, Joe found something he liked even better—his first Broadway show, which he saw as a guest of his friend Dorothy Earl and her mother, Rodgers and Hart's *A Connecticut Yankee in King Arthur's Court*. He described the musical extravaganza as "one of the great experiences of my life: to see how words and images could come to life that like." Infatuated, he pulled together whatever money he could save to buy tickets to more shows. Entering drama at school, he also appeared in the school's production of Gilbert and Sullivan's *H.M.S. Pinafore*, held at the prestigious Brooklyn Academy of Music. One of his teachers thought so highly of his performance that she recommended him to the American School of Dramatic Art, something he very much desired to pursue until he learned that the tuition cost $500, thus, ending his dream.

For Joe, his years at Erasmus Hall were, as he noted, "a time of discovery and of dreams without limits." He enjoyed every moment—the jammed-packed, boisterous football games and high school dances, and one unexpected surprise from someone so naturally creative: a love of prizefighting. He grew to like the sport after listening to the fights on radio, finding it glamorous and romantic, seduced by the raw power and the idea of two gladiator-like warriors pounding the living daylights out of each until only one was left standing.

In 1927, his senior year in high school, Joe enrolled in a boxing class, the first time it was offered. He sparred with his friends in his backyard after school and patterned his style after lightweight champion, Al Singer, after watching an 8-millimeter silent movie of his matches. He won all six bouts he fought at school, squaring off against an opponent his age—a kid named Toomey—for the lightweight championship at Erasmus Hall in front of Toomey's entire family. They watched, no doubt, in horror, as Joe pummeled him, winning the silver medal and championship.

After the match, Joe held his future in his hands. After his victory, a manager walked up to him and introduced himself. He was the manager of boxer Al Singer, and he offered to represent Joe. At that point, Singer was reportedly making $125,000 a year from boxing. Joe, then 16, accepted his offer. He trained at one of the most famous training of gyms in all of Manhattan with five rings of fighters. In one ring was none other than his idol, Al Singer, punching his sparring partner with lightning-quick fists.

In taking in the moment, eying managers, wearing expensive blue suits and pinkie rings puffing on their big cigars, and the smell of sweat and blood in the air, Joe listened to his inner voice: "I'm getting into this business at the wrong end." Seconds later, he walked out the door of the gym, never to pick up a boxing glove or fight another fight again.

In January 1928, Joe graduated early from Erasmus High—in three and a half years instead of four—with no interest in going to college. Pursuing a higher level of education took money, something he did not have in abundance. Besides, he was already involved with a girlfriend, his high school sweetheart Dorothy Earl, and the couple had become known in school as "Romeo and Juliet." He did not want to leave Dorothy behind for the sake of earning a college degree.

CHOOSING THE RIGHT PATH

After high school, Joe decided to become a banker instead. The proposition sounded attractive. This was a year and a half before the famous Wall Street stock market crash of 1929. But employment had already slowed to a crawl and there were no jobs. So Joe called in a favor. One of his father's customers, associated with the Irving Trust Bank, worked him into a position at the bank's main headquarters at 1 Wall Street in Lower Manhattan as a "racker" in the Rack Department. The job involved totaling incoming checks eight hours a day, using archaic and noisy devices to add them up correctly. But despite his incompetence, they promoted him to work in the Trust Department as an assistant tax man. Earning $16 a week, he worked with numbers, filling out and filing tax returns for some 400 trust accounts. Admittedly, Joe loathed every minute of the six years he spent working there and began looking for something else.

It was after a friend of his from Erasmus Hall asked him to draw portraits of some priests for the St. John's University yearbook and paid him $5 a piece for the portraits that Joe decided to become a cartoonist. He read and studied the humorous single-panel cartoons published in popular magazines of that day, including *Redbook*, *Saturday Evening Post*, and *Collier's*, and began drawing cartoons when the ideas struck him while living in an attic room that he rented in Flatbush. Disciplining himself with set working hours, he began to produce his cartoon ideas more rapidly. After much practice, he was able to sketch a drawing with just 10 strokes of the pen.

Consequently, Joe took the course of most cartoonists, submitting his completed cartoons to *Collier's*, *Redbook*, and the *Saturday Evening Post* during his lunch hour every Thursday when the clock struck noon. He would take his drawings and race down the stairs of the bank, take

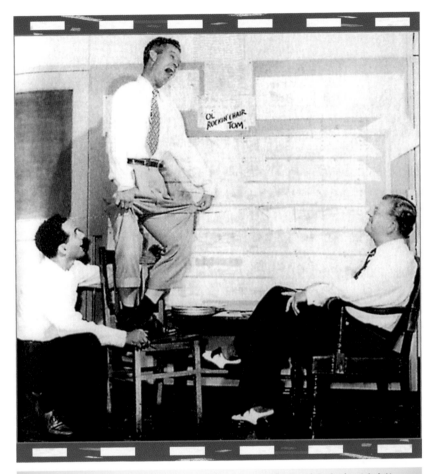

Joe (left) looks on in bemusement with producer Fred Quimby (right) as his partner Bill Hanna acts out in a hammy fashion the characters from the storyboard to their 1948 *Tom and Jerry* cartoon, *Old Rockin' Chair Tom.*

the subway, and drop off new drawings at the offices of each publication. As he once said in an interview, "Every day I left one pile of cartoons with a magazine while I dashed over to another to see if my previously submitted material had sold."

An inveterate doodler and dreamer, Joe kept drawing on the side, amassing a pile of "doodles" that he would continue to peddle during his lunch hour to all three publications. He continued the same cycle for two years, ending up with a pile of rejections. Despite the repeated rejections, Joe, a characteristically optimistic go-getter, never gave up. The Depression-era bootstrapper kept drawing to have, as he once said, "something to look forward to." Even if that was nothing more than drawing breath for a few moments in an office where people did something more than add, subtract, multiply, and divide, he continued making his daily rounds to publishing firms.

Then after countless rejections, the moment he had waited two long years for arrived. One Saturday, Joe received a letter from *Collier's* accepting one of his cartoons with a check for $25. It was the first check he had ever received; the bank paid all its employees in cash. It would not be the last. He sold three more cartoons to *Collier's*, then others to magazines like *Redbook* and *Saturday Evening Post*. His rash of success as an artist gave him a glimmer of hope that something more was out there for him professionally.

The turning point for Joe was in 1929, after the 18-year-old started selling his cartoons to *Collier's*, when he saw Walt Disney's landmark cartoon short *Skeleton Dance*, seated in the third balcony of the Roxy Theatre. Seeing the handiwork of Disney animator Ub Iwerks'-animated bone-clattering skeletons dancing across the screen in unison had a tremendous impact on him. "How do you do that?" he asked.

Joe left the theatre excited and, as satisfying as drawing cartoons for *Collier's* was, the prospects of doing animated cartoons—something that moved—was more exciting. Not much longer after seeing the Disney cartoon, he wrote animator Walt Disney, seeking advice on how to get started in the animation industry. Disney replied saying he would call the young would-be cartoonist during an upcoming trip to New York, but such a call never materialized. As Joe later noted in an interview, "The luckiest break I ever had was that he never called. I would have gone over there and disappeared."

Joe remained entranced with the art of animation, nonetheless. He took art classes at night at the Art Students League on 57th Street, costing him 50 cents a session. Afterward, he became more serious, enrolling in evening classes at the Pratt Institute in Brooklyn. After conversing about his desire to break into animation, his instructor arranged for him to meet with his former student, William Bowsky, then an animator at Fleischer Studios, home of the popular *Betty Boop* and *Popeye* theatrical cartoon series. During their meeting, Joe showed Bowsky samples of his four published *Colliers* cartoons. Impressed, Bowsky called him a day or so later, starting him at the bottom-rung position of painter in the ink and paint department coloring in black-and-white cels. Joe took a two-week vacation from his bank job and started. On his third day on the job, he was promoted to inker, a job involving tracing the original drawing with the acetate cel on top of it in ink. After hearing one his fellow inkers was stuck in the same position for three years without advancing, he quit that Thursday, went on a Bermuda cruise that Friday, and returned to work at the bank that Monday. As Joe said, "That was the end of my career in animation."

As fate would have it, Joe's dream of having a career in animation was far from over. In 1932, facing ever-worsening economic conditions, the Irving Trust Bank was forced to lay off many of its workers, retaining young, married employees with families to support instead of those who were single like Joe. Walking out the front door on his last day was like, as he once described, "the albatross had been lifted off my neck."

The following week after losing his bank job, Joe ran into a fraternity brother from Omega Alpha Pi, a fraternity from Erasmus Hall. After informing him about his predicament and his short-lived career at Fleischer Studios, his friend told him of a job opening at Van Beuren Studios, a small, independent cartoon studio and producer of low-quality theatrical cartoon shorts located on the 17th floor of the decaying United Artists building on 729 Seventh Avenue in the Bronx.

Armed with his portfolio of *Collier's* drawings, Joe walked in and applied for a job as an animator. He was hired on the spot by Jack Bogle, an artist who started his career drawing the *Felix the Cat* comic strip in 1927. Joe went to work as an in-betweener at a starting pay of $15 a week. There he learned the rudiments of animation. Every night after work, he would go home and practice drawing until the next morning. With his banking career now a distant memory, Joe was certain he had made the right decision. "Animation was something I truly wanted to do," he later recalled. "But it took me some time to figure out exactly if it would be worth it. Now I'm glad I did it."

MAKING A GOOD FIRST IMPRESSION

With a sincere determination to succeed, Joe worked his way up the ladder. Six months after he was hired, the studio, with a staff of about 150, promoted him to animator and storyboard artist. He ended up working on two theatrical sound cartoons distributed by RKO Pictures, *Cubby Bear*, launched in 1933, and *Rainbow Parades*, directed by former Disney animator Burt Gillett and others, which began a year later. He also co-produced the studio's most successful series, *Tom and Jerry*, starring two human cut-ups in amusing black-and-white adventures unrelated to his and Hanna's later, more successful cat-and-mouse creations.

In 1936, Joe married his high school sweetheart, Dorothy Earl, even though, in his words, they were "two very different people." They were married on a Friday and honeymooned that weekend at the famous Waldorf-Astoria hotel before he returned to work that Monday.

That same year, after Van Beuren lost its distribution contract with RKO, the studio was forced to shut down. Joe moved on to become an animator at Paul Terry's TerryToons Studio in New Rochelle, New York, joining his fellow Van Beuren cronies Dan Gordon and Jack Zander, where he worked on Terry's *Farmer Al Falfa* and *Kiko the Kangaroo* cartoons (which he aptly described as "some pretty dreadful stuff"). More than doing animation, he yearned to create stories of his own. So, after work, he drew up a storyboard for a *Kiko* cartoon involving a coast-to-coast air race with a handle-bar mustached baron he dreamed up called Dirty Doug. He submitted the finished storyboards to TerryToons director Manny Davis, who then showed them to Terry himself. Terry liked them enough that he hung them on the walls of his office, and that's as far as things went with Joe's storyboard creations.

After working at TerryToons Studio for around seven months, Joe became restless, itching for more out of his career than working in a place where he felt so dissatisfied, his only excitement having been over a few stories he had contributed. In 1937, one of his colleagues, a journeymen animator Ray Kelly, had heard from a friend in California that Metro-Goldwyn-Mayer was organizing a new cartoon studio and was seeking artists, animators, and story men. Offering animators $87.50 a week and a one-year contract to join, Kelly spread the word.

One by one, animators started bailing out of TerryToons like rats flee-ing the proverbial sinking ship. (Contrary to this story, his colleague Jack Zander remembered the chain of events differently in a letter, saying: "Had a call from Max Maxwell who said they were starting a cartoon department at MGM and could I help him with people. I rounded up Dan Gordon, Ray Kelly, Joe Barbera and Mike Meyers and we went to Calif. in the fall of 1937.")

Joe did the math: That was substantially more than what he was earning at TerryToons—a meager $55 a week, upped to $65 on his next payday—to work at a studio with markedly higher production values. On top of everything, California was, as he described, a virtual promise land of "eternal sunshine, balmy breezes . . . fresh air." He had little to lose.

By then, a year after his marriage, Joe and Dorothy had sepa-rated—the son of a Sicilian barber and a daughter of Irish descent prov-ing incompatible. She moved back to live with her parents while he returned to live with his mother. During their time apart, he still saw her, taking her out on occasion in his 1936 Ford roadster and then afterward returning to their respective homes. Still married but sepa-rated, they got along "better than we ever had before," but none of that changed his plans.

That summer, lured by the prospects of a better future with his car nose pointing west, Joe drove to California, taking three long weeks to get there, and never looked back. That June, Quimby hired him. And lit-tle did he realize at the time just how significant his career move would be and how he and another fellow MGM staffer would someday make history together.

3

Chasing Their Cartoon Dreams

Opening in late August of that year, MGM's new cartoon studio was initially headquartered in a house near the studio grounds. It was located at first in a modest building at Overland and Montana Avenues on MGM's Lot 2 next to its motion picture studio on its Culver City lot. Put in charge of this promising new group was a nattily dressed, benevolent and refined 51-year-old business man, Fred Quimby, who had worked in the film business since 1913, first with Pathé, a leading film equipment and production company in the early 20th century. After a three-year stint with Fox Studios, in 1926, he joined MGM to become head of sales and distribution for its short-feature department. In 1937, after many years of distinguished service, the studio promoted him to short films department chief, giving him special supervision over cartoons.

In establishing MGM's new Cartoon Department, the Minneapolis, Minnesota native raided top talent from every major American animation studio, including Harman-Ising, Columbia Pictures, TerryToons, Warner Bros., and Leon Schlesinger Productions. Among the contingent of animators and story men recruited from New York to join the studio, Joe was put to work as an animator and story man. Little did he realize that one day before his arrival, another talented animator would be among the first wave of new employees to report to the studio as a newly hired director whose desk would be opposite his. His name was William Hanna.

For Bill, the first day of his arrival was "like a high school reunion," since many former Harman-Ising animators, along with another local Columbia Pictures defector, Emery Hawkins, were hired by producer Quimby for the studio's core animation unit. His second day, he met the New Yorkers who ventured west to complete Quimby's cartoon studio, including Dan Gordon, George Gordon, Ray Kelly, Paul Sommer, and one dynamic, dark-haired and exuberant Joseph Barbera, who impressed him with his speed and drawing ability. As his fellow colleague and animator Jack Zander, who also was hired, once related, "He could draw a storyboard so fast that it would take two people to pin the drawings up on the board while he was making them."

Working in close quarters, from the first day of his employment, Bill and his colleagues became aware of the kind of boss Quimby was. He lacked a sense of humor and understanding of animation production. He was not indifferent, but he left the creativity up to his animators and saw his job as making sure "we got it done" before distributing it to theaters. Unlike their boss, the department of 20-something animators were much more informally dressed, wearing slacks and shirt-sleeves and thoroughly engrossed in their work. As Bill wrote in his autobiography, *A Cast of Friends*, "We were challenged to be more than artists and animators working at our drawing boards. If we did our jobs right, we would be creating the architecture of a young studio that would become a major contender in commercial animation."

As the studio's first cartoon series out the gate, MGM purchased between August to October of that year the rights to creator Rudolph Dirks's famous United Feature Syndicate comic-strip, *The Katzenjammer Kids*, renaming it *Captain and the Kids*. Quimby assigned Bill and studio newcomers Friz Freleng and Bob Allen to helm individual cartoons in the new series. It was Bill's second try at directing since his one-film stint at the helm at Harman-Ising Studios a year earlier. Freleng was a veteran director who came over from Warner Bros. after his long success directing *Merrie Melodies* and *Looney Tunes*; Allen, previously an animator, was new to cartoon directing. Among those serving on Freleng's unit was Joe Barbera, a man brimming with ideas and clever cartoon gags but whose talent became wasted among a sea of other unit animators toiling on the series.

CAPTAINING A SINKING SHIP

Bill had "misgivings" from the start about adapting "the ponderously drawn human characters . . . with German accents" into an animated form, as did Freleng, Leon Schlesinger's former top director at Warner Bros., who was far more blunt in his criticism about the studio's decision to use the strip but to no avail. The studio thought that because the comic strip was published in so many newspapers across the country it would become a popular film cartoon as well.

Like its famed comic-strip predecessor, the animated *Captain and the Kids* series depicted the misadventures of a family of German immigrants—the Captain, who spoke hardly any English; Mamma, the Captain's wife; and their two insufferable offspring, Hans and Fritz—and the Captain's bumbling friend, the Inspector, in single-reel adventures originally intended to be filmed in three-strip Technicolor. With budgets at MGM twice as much as those at Warner Bros., the top studio brass balked at the idea. To save money, they filmed the cartoons in black and white and released them in sepia tone; only two of the 15 cartoon shorts were later shot in Technicolor.

On April 2, 1938, Bill's first cartoon as a series director and second of the series, *Blue Monday*, debuted in theaters. The story has the grumpy Captain arising on a Monday morning. He accuses Mamma (that's Mrs. Katzenjammer) of "poorly managing the household." With that remark, Mamma puts the Captain in charge of vacuuming the house, washing the clothes, and other chores. Finishing these odd jobs with the incapable assistance of the Inspector, Mamma returns home only to find the house in shambles. Like many cartoons in the series, *Blue Monday* opened to mixed reviews. Despite lukewarm critical reception, the cartoon provided Bill with a new challenge: supervising one more cartoon that year, a rollicking adventure of the Captain and a lion, titled *What a Lion!*

Producing winning cartoons with any consistency became a huge challenge. After completing his third or fourth cartoon in the series, the 28-year-old animator realized he needed to develop a good character of his own, or with a partner, who had the quality skills he lacked (he concluded after years in the business that he was "a lousy artist"), and that would be more professionally fulfilling. But at the time, as much as MGM's cartoon studio was brimming with talent, Bill never considered he might eventually partner with Joseph Barbera until fate intervened.

Joe, meanwhile, was unhappy working on the *Captain and the Kids* series as well. Of the comic-strip-turned-cartoon, he said it was like "enduring a five-minute ordeal" and that seemed "anything but funny." In late 1937, he became so depressed over his situation that he called his estranged wife, Dorothy, still living in Brooklyn, to tell her, "I'm coming home." She talked him out it and he stayed, more determined than ever to make things happen for his career. Lonely without each other, despite their past marital misgivings, they agreed to live together. She moved west and after four weeks of cohabitating together, Joe ended the marriage once and for all. But as she was preparing to return to New York, she announced surprising news: She was pregnant. Unable to shed the prevailing mores of that time or his Sicilian upbringing, Joe remained married to her.

Restricted by weak stories and primitive animation, Bill did a capable job of directing. Early reports from the field from theater owners passed on to Quimby were that the *Captain and the Kids* were simply "not getting the laughs" from movie audiences. While some were mildly entertaining, most were "merely boring." At issue besides the humor was the fact the films lacked appealing characters who possessed, as Bill had learned from his years working with Harman and Ising, "a kind of visual cartoon charisma" or "cuteness" that was endearing to audiences. Despite larger budgets, a brand-new production facility, and a talented and experienced crew, the series became an abject failure.

By the summer of 1938, Quimby and the studio brass became aware that its fledgling cartoon studio was floundering. Critical pans and box-office receipts told the story. The *Captain and the Kids* did not provide the box-office sizzle for which they had hoped; instead, it fizzled. Before incurring much more damage to the studio's reputation and financial bottom line, Quimby canceled the series. By this point, Friz Freleng had returned to Warner Bros. after Leon Schlesinger upped his salary to $250 a week, even though it was less than what he had made at MGM.

The studio brass did not help matters much. Coinciding with production of its ill-fated *Captain and the Kid* series, they made yet another questionable move. On March 11, 1938, they hired, behind Quimby's back, revered newspaper cartoonist and columnist Harry Hershfield, with virtually no animation experience, to head the Cartoon Department's story department and adapt his most famous and longest-running strip, *Abie the Agent*, for animation. Hershfield later commented of his hiring, "They were so glad to welcome me, the day I arrived they gave me a farewell dinner."

Hershfield's arrival only added to the already tense working environment with the studio putting him in charge of the department over Quimby, certainly not a vote of confidence in Quimby's ability to still steer the ship. The longtime studio executive was so nonplussed he did everything in his power to get Hershfield fired. "He arranged a showdown meeting with Hershfield, the studio brass, and us, 'the creative people.' It was one of those brutal events you read about as typical of Hollywood's 'Golden Age,'" Joe later wrote. "Quimby went around the room, demanding from each of us a recitation of grievances. The result was Hershfield's removal, the crystallization of a fresh batch of hard feelings, and our deliverance wholly into the hands of Fred Quimby."

In blending artists from both coasts, such personality conflicts seemed inevitable. As Joe, one of about eight New Yorkers Quimby had brought west, stated, "...the situation deteriorated daily. Not only did we lack good material, we were plagued by personality conflicts, beginning with a basic geographical-cultural incompatibility between the Westerners and the Easterners. Within a few months, one by one, they all returned east—except for me." Bill, on the other hand, who worked mostly with members of the New York faction, offered a much different view: "I had a very high regard for most of the New York group that was there and enjoyed being there with them."

In early October 1938, to do something to pull MGM's Cartoon Department out of the abyss, the studio announced they had rehired two experienced hands to return to the studio lot, Bill's old bosses Harman and Ising. Signing them to a seven-year agreement, they would work directly under the studio's control while remaining independent producers to produce at least eight cartoons a year, with their unit operating under Quimby's supervision.

Subsequently, the studio also brought on board another renowned newspaper cartoonist to bolster the reputation of its flagging Cartoon Department and inject some life into its *Captain and the Kids* series and create their own cartoon shorts: Milt Gross. Gross had created the popular strip *Phool Phan Phables*; and written, produced, and directed a silent cartoon based on the strip, *The Ups & Downs of Mr. Phool Phan* (1918), as well as dozens more cartoons during the silent era for producer J. R. Bray. He was hardly the same man when he arrived at MGM. In ill-health with a heart condition, he routinely joked that "Yeah, someday a waiter will find my head in the soup. Pick my head up by the hair and say, 'He's had enough.'"

Gross suffered the same fate as Hershfield, not because of his heart but due to his increasing paranoia. Situated right next to Quimby's office, Gross struggled to hear through the grillwork heat register what Quimby was saying about him. As a result, his return to animated cartoons was brief. His work on the *Captain and the Kids* series went largely uncredited. He did, however, revive his *Count Screwloose* comic-strip characters—Count Screwloose and J. R. the Wonder Dog—in two shorts he directed, both released in 1939: *Jitterbug Follies* (February 25) and *Wanted: No Master* (March 18). Besides the fact that his zany style of humor clashed with Quimby's more dignified and reserved approach, Gross flipped his lid, as Joe remembered, "going through the studio firing everybody," so Quimby fired him.

Before dumping the *Captain and the Kids* series, MGM produced three new cartoons in 1939: *Petunia National Park, Seal Skinners,* and

Mamma's New Hat. Since at this point the series was dead on arrival, some theater managers, who routinely screened the series, withdrew from screening the final cartoons. Some replaced them with the studio's new Harman and Ising cartoons instead.

Amidst the maelstrom of activity, that year marked an important event in Bill's life: On January 3, he and Violet witnessed the arrival of their first-born child, a son, David. Three years later, on January 27, 1942, they would give him a playmate, a sister, Bonnie, making their family complete.

TEAMING UP AND DEVELOPING A FAMOUS CAT AND MOUSE

With Harman and Ising at the helm, Bill and Joe were assigned to work under them in the story department. Describing them as both "amiable people and bosses," Joe, unlike Bill, found working under them—Harman, a man of high artistic ideals who wanted to "raise cartoons to loftier heights," and Ising, notoriously indecisive—challenging, to say the least. While a self-starter, Ising "seemed acutely afflicted with an ability to make a decision." As a result, during story meetings, Ising, always more concerned about how a character was drawn, would puff on a cigarette and draw out the process. Consequently, storyboarding a single cartoon took six months under his direction.

The musical chairs at MGM's cartoon studio created the golden opportunity both Bill and Joe had waited for. In late August 1939, Quimby put them in charge of a third cartoon unit, increasing the department's annual output of musical cartons from 15 to 18 with the addition of their unit that was to function as a supplement to Harman and Ising's two units. Meanwhile, Quimby also allowed his group of animators to develop new, original cartoon characters of their own. Their desks opposite of each other, they quickly fused into a dynamic team—Bill, with his keen eye for tempo and timing, and Joe, a lightning-fast draftsman and clever story and gagman—and developed a close rapport. As Bill noted in his autobiography, "Joe's remarkable artistic talents were apparent to me from our first introduction. I could

Drawing names from a hat from a studio contest they held, Bill and Joe named their characters, Tom and Jerry. © *Metro-Goldwyn-Mayer Inc.*

see that he possessed the ability to capture the mood and expression in a quick sketch better than anyone else I knew. He also was brimming with ideas for working up clever gags which appealed to my own sense of humor." As Joe later added, "We understood each other and had a mutual respect for each other's work."

While Ising began developing a new cartoon character to introduce to the screen, the lovable and lumbering Barney Bear, Bill and Joe took seriously the task of creating characters of lasting value. Joe, who was certain the studio was on the verge of shutting its doors, said to Bill, "Why don't we do a cartoon on our own?" They bounced ideas off each other. They considered many different combinations of characters and natural adversaries—a dog and cat, or bird and cat—and intrinsic characteristics that would spark conflict and humor between them. As Bill remembered, "We asked ourselves what would be a normal conflict between characters provoking comedy while retaining a basic situation from which we could continue to generate plots and stories." They settled on a cat and a mouse.

After discussing the idea further, they believed they had a winning formula on their hands. The very idea of "a little mouse" chasing, tormenting, brutalizing, and demoralizing a "big nasty cat," with the waifish mouse always ending up the winner, seemed magical. In Joe's words, "I knew that no matter where you ran with it, the minute you saw a cat and a mouse you knew it was a chase."

When they informed Harman and Ising and their colleagues of what they were developing, they were greeted with an unenthusiastic, "A cat and a mouse! How unoriginal can you get?" The fact was many other studios had done cat and mouse cartoons in some form or another, but none like what they were proposing. Joe later added, "Now I can't honestly say Bill and I thought we were going to make the world sit up and take notice . . . What we *were* sure of, though, is that we wouldn't do any worse than anyone else at the studio." Ising, who supervised their work, was originally supposed to direct the film, but as Joe writes, he "didn't want anything to do with it, figuring we would go down the drain very nicely on our own."

After drafting a story and making a few quick sketches, they presented their idea to Quimby. He was not crazy about the idea. It was his opinion that cat and mouse cartoons had been done too many times. "What can you do with a cat and mouse that would be different?" Quimby asked. They told him to give them a chance to show him the idea could work. Without further interference, he did.

Joe developed a series of preliminary pencil sketches of the characters—a mangy, moonfaced, menacing cat named Jasper and a wide-eyed, diminutive, mischievous mouse, Jinx—demonstrating a variety of poses and expressions that Bill said were "among the most appealing in animation that I had ever seen."

For the next two months, they developed an original story featuring both characters and consisting mostly of gags and action that Joe then used to draw full-size layouts instead of storyboards. The result of their first collaboration was a cartoon titled *Puss Gets the Boot*. Instead of pitching their idea as a storyboard, the usual step in the process of presenting a new idea to garner support, they decided to produce a demonstration film. Taking their conceptual drawings, they produced seven-minute prototype, filming Joe's full-size layouts in sequence—fewer than 1,800 drawings, much less than the number of drawings routinely used to produce a fully animated cartoon. "We did every frame of that first cartoon," Bill stated.

Once completed, they previewed the film on a Movieola in a studio projection room for MGM studio executives. A few minutes into the film, the place erupted with uncontrollable howls of laughter as they watched Bill and Joe's two precocious offspring light up the screen in a series of rollicking and outrageous chases that left a positive impression on everyone, including the usually stodgy Quimby. As a result, Bill and Joe were given the green light to direct the actual cartoon, supposedly under Ising's supervision. Production soon got underway and they hoped the film would become the basis for a continuing series of adventures that they could codirect.

Much to Bill and Joe's surprise, unlike with their test film, Quimby and other executives acted with "utter indifference" to the final product. Joe wrote in his autobiography that the release of *Puss Gets the Boot* was not "treated as anything special. It was just dumped in the theaters."

That changed once the public saw the film. The response was overwhelmingly positive. On February 10, 1940, *Puss Gets the Boot* made its debut in movie theaters across the country, enjoying a six-week run in Los Angeles and becoming a resounding success with critics and moviegoers alike. Audiences roared with laughter and cheered over the filmed antics (as Joe added, "You'd hear a yell in the theater— 'Wow!'") of the seemingly innocent mouse, Jinx, and his long-tailed house cat, Jasper, wreaking havoc and setting off a path of destruction in their wake.

In this introductory short, Jasper and Jinx are a typical house cat and mischievous mouse trying to outsmart one another. In doing so, Jasper crashes into a planter, splintering it into pieces and getting warned by the black housekeeper, Mammy Two-Shoes, if he breaks one more thing, he will be banished from the household for good and be an outdoor cat. Jinx, perfectly primed and ready for mischief, does his best to make that a reality. He runs through the house throwing every breakable object to the floor he can get his hands on—glasses and dishes—as an exasperated Jasper, remembering Mammy Two-Shoes's famous parting words, makes a madcap attempt to stop him from breaking everything in sight. A seesaw battle ensues with comically disastrous results before Jasper gets the boot.

Until then, critics had never seen anything like Jinx and Jasper and loved the new pair, garnering favorable reviews from the trades. The *Motion Picture Herald* praised *Puss Gets the Boot* as "an especially clever portrayal of the smug superiority of the cat dictator" oblivious to the fact the mouse, Jasper, was the superior one, becoming, as Joe described, "far and away the most successful cartoon MGM had yet released." One thing they discovered in making their cat-and-mouse characters' debut short, as Bill once explained, was "the harder they hit, the louder they laugh. So we didn't change our formula."

Conspicuous by their absence was the fact neither Bill nor Joe received onscreen credits as the film's director. Only Rudolf Ising is credited at the beginning of the film ("A Rudolf Ising Production"), making it seem that he alone conceived the characters and the plot and directed the story when the opposite was true. In an article published on May 26, 1940, three months after the film's release, Associated Press reporter Hubbard Keavy reported the stunning omission. He stated: "A very entertaining cartoon making the rounds now deserves some belated attention . . . At the beginning it states a man named Ising produced the picture for M.G.M., but more than one person wondered who conceived the characters and the plot and directed the story. I was one, and, in addition, told it with such simplicity it will not confuse children—nor bore adults. The answer is a pair of young fellows, Joe Barbera . . . and Bill Hanna." Keavy predicted, however, because of the success of *Puss*, their names would appear "in large letters on every picture they make."

At the time of Keavy's article, Bill and Joe, who expected to direct six cartoons that year, were already hard at work on their fifth picture, *Gallopin' Gals*. However, despite feeling assured of their positions as directors, a single phone call almost derailed their partnership from beginning in earnest. One day, Joe received a surprise call from former colleague Friz Freleng, who was directing cartoons at Warner Bros. Freleng wanted to meet with him that Sunday. Though a day he reserved for the Sabbath, Joe drove over to the Warner's lot and Freleng did not waste any time recruiting him. He offered to beat his current salary at MGM if he came over as an animator, story man, director, or, as Joe put it, "whatever I wanted to be."

Given his rising status at MGM and the launch of the *Tom and Jerry* series, Joe was conflicted over the situation. He talked himself out of the opportunity and turned Freleng down. In the meantime, that Monday, Quimby got wind of what went down and asked Joe, "Is it true?"

Without hesitation, Joe told him yes.

Quimby countered, "I'll match their offer."

At the time, Joe was earning $100 a week; Freleng had offered him $125. Joe agreed and he and Quimby shook hands on the deal.

While ecstatic over the reception of their joint film, Quimby, a humorless movie executive whose staff artistically succeeded in spite of him, felt otherwise. He called them into his office and said, "I don't want you to make anymore pictures with the cat and mouse."

Bill and Joe were stunned and one of them asked, "Why?"

The bespectacled Quimby did not mince words. "We don't want to put all our eggs in one basket."

OVERCOMING CREATIVE INDIFFERENCE

Subsequently, Quimby dispatched the talented pair to codirect a quadruplet of "terrible cartoons" distributed under the MGM banner instead. Making these films was like being in cartoon purgatory, knowing full well they had the potential to do better work with characters—Jasper and Jinx—the public loved. Stylistically, the films were drawn like Harman and Ising and Disney cartoons of this era— slickly rendered and handsomely animated. The first cartoon they directed, issued to theaters in mid-May, was *Swing Social*. It stars a preacher who tells a moonshine-packing black fisherman fishing off a pier the unbelievable tale of why fish do not bite on Sundays. Panning down to the watery depths below, a school of catfish in blackface are seen performing swing numbers of popular stars of the day. That April, they helmed their second cartoon, *The Goose Goes South*, a how-to/ travelogue spoof cobbled together by a series of blackout jokes, or succession of gags, starring nondescript characters. A little goose walks south instead of flying, hitchhiking as he goes. He runs into trouble with a family of hillbillies for trespassing. He also runs into a bird caricature of popular singer Kate Smith, Southern pinball players, and, in a recurring gag, a driver who stops, then speaks gibberish as his reasoning for not giving him a lift.

The third among this group, arriving in theaters in early September, was *Officer Pooch*, starring an ice-cream-swilling cop who tries rescuing a kitten caught on top of a utility pole while a stray mutt muscles in on his territory by trying to snatch the same cat. In late October, their fourth non-cat-and-mouse effort was the aforementioned Technicolor one-shot *Gallopin' Gals*. The one-reel short features gossiping mares pitted opposite a clumsy 100-to-1 long shot, Maggie, who ends up winning her first horse race despite seemingly impossible odds.

After such unrewarding sideshows in cartoon making, Bill and Joe went ahead with directing a second cat-and-mouse cartoon. Before proceeding, however, they were convinced they needed a better name for their animated pair. Rather than choose the names themselves, they sponsored a contest inviting studio personnel to submit their suggestions on pieces of paper that they tossed into a hat. From hundreds of names, they shook the names in a hat and pulled out every suggestion passing over 50 times the name they settled on, "Tom and Jerry," submitted by animator John Carr and who was awarded $50 prize money.

After renaming the dueling cat and mouse, Bill and Joe went to the powers-that-be to tell them the good news that they had a new cartoon—a *Tom and Jerry* cartoon—in the works. The reaction was again one of indifference—still of the mindset, "Too many cat and mouse cartoons," with little new or entertaining to offer in any combination or form. As hard as they tried, they could not convince the "suits" otherwise and the future of Tom and Jerry appeared to remain in limbo.

Two coinciding events would influence the course of history. Despite being released with relatively little fanfare, *Puss Gets the Boot* had generated a much more enthusiastic response than MGM executives had counted on. Praise continued to pour in, as a result. Quimby received a letter from a woman of obvious clout, Besa Short, a film exhibitor and owner of the Loew's theater chain in Dallas, Texas, expressing her admiration for the film and inquiring, "When are we going to see more of these charming cat-and-mouse cartoons?" Besides becoming widely embraced by film exhibitors like Short, that spring, Bill and Joe drew the highest honor possible from their peers for their first effort: an Academy Award nomination for "Best Short-Subject (Cartoon)." As a result, Quimby and the studio brass conceded, giving Bill and Joe the okay to direct two more *Tom and Jerry* cartoons starring the dueling cat-and-mouse duo.

Although technically they were supervised by Ising, Quimby's plan was to develop Bill and Joe into their own production unit independent from Harman and Ising, with whom, as Joe writes, "he [Quimby] was constantly at odds." Of the two, Bill felt a deep loyalty to Ising dating back to his days at Harman-Ising studios. His conscience got the better part of him. After returning from a brief vacation, Joe discovered that Bill had lobbied Quimby, unbeknownst to him, for them to work under Ising. Quimby called them in to meet with him and discuss Bill's proposition. After stating he understood they were willing to work under Ising, Joe flat out stated, "I don't know why we would do that, because Rudy never came into the room when we were doing 'Puss.'"

In Joe's words, Quimby worked "himself into a loose-dentured rage," barking, "Are you telling me that Rudy never came into the room?"

Joe confirmed it.

"Is that right, Bill?"

Bill answered, "Yes."

"Well, then. I'm not about to give him credit for these pictures. You just keep going along the way you are."

Like their newly christened characters, Bill and Joe would be off and running again, this time producing what became one of the most successful theatrical cartoon series in the annals of movie history.

Fathering Filmdom's Most Famous Cat and Mouse

With the backing of the studio, it was full speed ahead as Bill and Joe embarked on directing the first "official" *Tom and Jerry* cartoon, *The Midnight Snack*. For this second short, they modified the physical appearance of their characters—making them less homey—and added another dimension to the mix: developing a relationship between them. They also determined from the outset the kind of chemistry necessary for the characters—neither of whom talked—to communicate through the physical action and draw out their distinctive personalities—the wily, hot-tempered menace, Tom, and the mischievous, clever, chubby-cheeked Jerry. This, as Bill once said, "put them in a league all of their own."

Employing much improved gag material over *Puss Gets the Boot*, *The Midnight Snack* got the *Tom and Jerry* franchise off to a fast and glorious start. Released on July 19, 1941, the two characters skirmish over refrigerator privileges, with Jerry becoming trapped in the icebox, as discovered by the recurring character Mammy Two-Shoes, a plump, black housemaid (voiced by actress Lillian Randolph). Audiences only got occasional glimpses of her physical form in 18 cartoon shorts altogether. In the end, through some fancy maneuvering on Tom's part, Jerry winds up in the freezer with horrified Mammy Two-Shoes once again giving her house cat the boot.

That December, as part of the studio's two-picture approval, Bill and Joe codirected in time for Christmas their second *Tom and Jerry* short, *The Night Before Christmas.* In this hilarious holiday film, while frolicking under the Christmas tree, Tom finds more than wrapped presents—his little friend Jerry, who guiles the temperamental tabby into chasing him after Jerry tries to make peace with mistletoe. The film marks the first time the bluish-gray tabby shows he has a conscience after barricading Jerry outside in the cold and freezing snow. Academy voters handed the film Bill and Joe's second nomination for an Academy Award for "Best Short-Subject (Cartoon)," a unique triumph.

FINDING A SYSTEM THAT WORKED

After Hugh Harman left in 1941 to form his own company and Rudolf Ising left a year later, only two animation units remained—Bill and Joe's and that of Tex Avery, known for his over-the-top screwball cartoons at Warner Bros., who had joined the studio in 1942. From Tom and Jerry's official launch in 1941, Bill and Joe developed a solid foundation—making only subtle changes to the personalities and looks of their two stars over the years. They also developed a production system that contributed to their success and mostly remained in check for the next 16 years. Bill and Joe usually held bull sessions, tossing ideas and suggestions back and forth for possible stories. Bill, the more soft-spoken of the two, responded, "That's swell," if he liked an idea, or "That smells," if he did not. Sometimes their idea started only as a title for the cartoon before they built a story around it. Joe would sketch while Bill talked, drawing little thumbnail sketches as fast as they discussed them. His quick, unpolished drawings would become the basis of the storyboard on which a film script would be written, with Joe writing the finished story.

Bill then timed the entire picture using oversized timing or expo-sure sheets, divided into four long columns, indicating how many draw-ings or frames were required for each frame of action before animators animated them. Afterward, he passed on the storyboard and exposure sheets to their versatile layout artist Richard Bickenbach to produce the actual layouts of the film. Once completed, using the storyboards, expo-sure sheets, and layouts, Bill would hold a production meeting and act out in a loud, exaggerated, and "very hammy fashion" different gags, facial expressions, and physical movements of the characters and scenes for animators Irven Spence, Ed Barge, Ken Muse, and Ray Patterson to give them a much better sense and feel for the cartoon before animating it. In many cases, as Bill noted, "These dramatizations often carried over into the actual production," including the different extreme character-izations Bill acted out for them. As Spence related, "Bill could really get the expressions on Tom and Jerry and my gosh, you knew what they wanted after this little meeting."

Bill and Joe recorded most of the vocal effects with a sound engi-neer in the booth in advance of animators commencing on the actual animation. Under Joe's direction, Bill produced synchronized vocals—screeches or yowls—for Tom and sometimes Jerry (as did other voice actors infrequently) that were kept intact in the films' actual soundtracks.

In creating the animation, Bill and Joe divvied up the work accord-ing to each animator's specialty. Spence, Bill's longtime friend since high school, mostly animated the frenzied action scenes or those requiring added "effects," like a tomato splattering on a wall. Barge, another Har-man and Ising transplant like Hanna, handled more general animation, while Muse provided the personal touches and reaction shots of the characters' distinctive personalities. Patterson, who joined MGM after working at Disney, had a knack for animating mush-mouth dialogue and a peculiarly spiky way of handling action, with Bill crediting both Spence and him for mostly "setting tone for the personality animation" in the series.

Each was assigned 100 to 150 feet of animation—an average of 25 feet a week—to produce for a whole sequence, roughly around six weeks of work. After all the drawings were refined, cleaned up, and completed,

Bill and Joe would flip through the entire stack, examining their overall smoothness and characterizations, and have their animators redo any to perfection before producing a pencil test from the storyboards to preview before producing the finished cartoon. Such "rehearsals" cost about $3,000 to produce. Sometimes they would have their animators redo specific scenes as many as four times. Such precision was necessary to catch the right expression, tighten up the timing of a gag, or squash and stretch animation of the character or action. Once approved, the sequences were then sent to the Ink and Paint Department to ink and color each scene and paint the backgrounds before being sent to the Camera Department to photograph the actual theatrical color cartoon.

By "getting the bugs out," Bill and Joe were able to produce their cartoons at a savings—an average of $25,000, compared to the usual costs for a one-reel cartoon from $30,000 to $35,000. This was partly due to the fact that their films, unlike more arty cartoons stressing color and odd camera angles, featured simple characters animated against simple, unpretentious backgrounds. As Joe stated at the time, "The idea is to make them funny. The purpose of the cartoon is to make people laugh. That's all we're trying to do."

In the absence of characters that never talked (with a few minor exceptions), Bill and Joe enlisted the studio's talented and creative musical director, Scott Bradley, to produce a swift brand of music to set the mood and playful humor throughout each cartoon. Joining MGM's new in-house Cartoon Department in 1937, the blond-haired, small-statured, former Harman-Ising composer wrote and arranged complex music and melodies. Supervising a studio orchestra of 16 to 30 musicians, his scores combined elements of jazz, classical, and pop music as well as MGM hit songs and old favorites—"The Trolley Song," a Bradley standard in virtually every film, from *Meet Me in St. Louis* (1944) starring Judy Garland; "Sing Before Breakfast," from the *Broadway Medley of 1936*; and many others among his orchestrations. Many of the series' Oscar-winning and nominated shorts were enhanced by Bradley's melodic orchestral arrangements.

Besides the inherent chemistry of Tom and Jerry on screen, the chemistry between Bill and Joe and their animation team was equally good off screen. Working in a relaxed production environment allowed them to experiment and work on a more "trial-and-error" basis, unlike studios where animators did not always have such a luxury. Calling his unit animators "one of the most gifted animation production teams I have ever known," Bill later commented that a true sense of ". . . camaraderie pervaded the whole studio, and I think most of us shared a general feeling of goodwill for the prospects of anyone working on Lot 2 regardless of what their job was."

With such a high-spirited and rambunctious group of professionals, mostly in their twenties and thirties, pulling practical jokes or pranks in some fashion was often the order of the day. Often Joe was the biggest prankster, rigging buckets of water on transoms to drench unsuspecting victims entering the studio, or instigating pushpin and spitball fights. Other times, they took their skirmishes outside on the studio back lot. They would play touch football games on a large grassy lawn, with Bill refereeing as Joe produced spectacular running plays for his team. One reason their partnership lasted as long as it did was they rarely saw each other outside of work, keeping their professional and private lives separate.

By 1940, after buying a five-acre, undeveloped plot of walnut trees in the San Fernando Valley intending to build a home there, Bill, then earning $175 a week at MGM, and Violet traded the property for a lot in Sherman Oaks. They broke ground and completed construction that year on a ranch-styled family home, a mere 30-minute drive to the studio, where they would live and raise their two children.

Conversely, Joe's marriage to Dorothy remained a rocky affair. Nearly separating several years earlier, they stayed together after discovering she was pregnant with their first child, a daughter they named Lynn. Dorothy then gave birth on November 10, 1941, to a second daughter, Jayne. They rented a small house complete with a black-widow-infested garage in Westwood for $40 a month before Joe bought a lot in the nearby high-rent district of Brentwood for $1,850—with exactly $2,000 in the bank—and built a brand-new house, playing, as he described, "the role of dutiful suburban pater familias." Three years later, on July 25, 1944, they would welcome a third arrival, a son, Neal Francis.

MASTERING CAT-AND-MOUSE GAMES

At Metro, Bill and Joe would direct an extraordinary 114 *Tom and Jerry* cartoons overall through the late 1950s, an average of six to seven shorts per year, with plots, as animation writer Mark Mayerson wrote, that were essentially "a new twist on an old story." Throughout this period, they took their highly orchestrated slapstick comedy to extraordinary new heights, dominating the Oscars in the animated shorts category. Between 1943 and 1954, they netted a record additional 12 Oscar nominations, winning seven times—the most ever for a single series in motion picture history, becoming most honored animators during Hollywood's "golden age of animation."

Their films only got funnier as they honed their skills and developed their famous cat-and-mouse characters. The trendsetter was their 11th *Tom and Jerry* cartoon, *Yankee Doodle Mouse.* The war-time short, issued to theaters on June 26, 1943, provides Fourth of July fireworks, the kind only Tom and Jerry can create. Living in a cellar of a stolid, suburban home, Jerry, sporting a bottle-cap helmet, uses blitz tactics and an ingenious arsenal of "hen-grenades," a banana-throwing catapult, and lightbulb bombs, to punish Tom, who is protected only by a succession of homemade helmets and bunkers and barricades, before shooting the helpless house cat up into the heavens, where he explodes into a sparkling display of red, white, and blue–hued fireworks shaped like the American flag.

Both film critics and their peers lauded Bill and Joe's latest entry. In fact, that same year, they were awarded their first Oscar for "Best Short-Subject" (Cartoon)." Not since Rudolf Ising took the award in 1940 for *The Milky Way* had MGM won an Academy Award for its animated cartoons. Bill and Joe became only the second in the studio's history to receive the award.

Winning the Oscar did little to change their relationship with their boss, Fred Quimby, in persuading him to sign off on their ideas for subsequent films. Anytime they tried talking to him about a new *Tom and Jerry* cartoon in progress, "reeling off the gags, and dancing around to indicate some of the action," as Joe recalled, he usually stopped them at mid-sentence and said, "You don't have to tell me anything. I know what you're thinking before you even tell me."

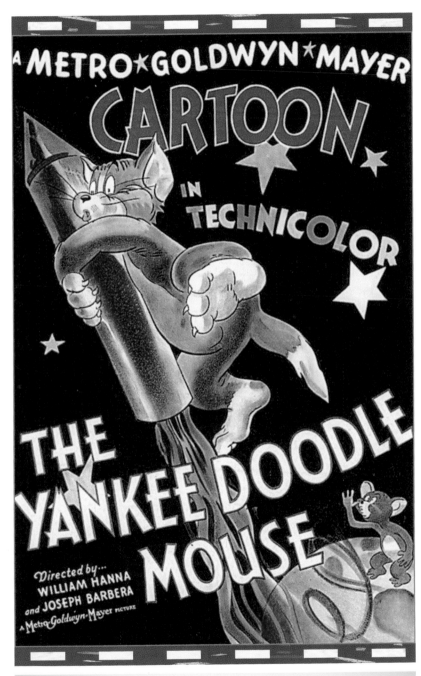

Poster art to Bill and Joe's first Oscar-winning *Tom and Jerry* short, *Yankee Doodle Mouse* (1943). © *Metro-Goldwyn-Mayer Inc.*

Essentially, he abstained from having any further responsibility in listening to their ideas.

As the pair started winning more Oscars, Quimby was the one who took the stage and basked in the glory, claiming such honors on their behalf, as they looked on from afar during the awards ceremony. This was because the Academy's policy prohibited those creatively involved in the production from accepting the award. Since they were credited as directors and Quimby as the producer, he was designated to accept the honors even though he had contributed nothing to each film's creation. They begged him to award them coproducer credit to make them eligible, but he told him his hands were tied and that then-MGM vice president and general manager Eddie Mannix would not like it. Quimby's insecurity reared its ugly head again. When the studio started rereleasing their *Tom and Jerry* cartoons, he inserted onto new prints full-screen credit as producer and credited Bill and Joe as writers and directors—in Joe's words, "precisely what he had condemned Rudy Ising for doing."

Years later, they were awarded their seventh Oscar. While Quimby was off at a meeting, Bill and Joe conspired together to get their payback. They gathered their animators—Irv Spence, Ken Muse, Ed Barge, and Dick Bickenbach—in Quimby's office behind his desk and snapped a "conspiratorial photograph" of them all grinning with all seven golden statuettes as a memento.

Whenever major film exhibitors dropped in at the studio, Quimby typically took them on a tour showing off how their cartoons were made. But after bringing so many through, he stopped, concerned the studio brass upstairs would realize who was really behind their making. In fact, one day, he took Bill and Joe outside and told them, "You know something, you fellows are too important to be disturbed like this. I'm not going to bother you with any more visitors."

Their success notwithstanding, Bill's line of work did little to impress his two children, David and Bonnie, either. As he later remembered, "Their dad simply headed for the office every day like any other father and came home every evening after work," and they never displayed much curiosity about what he did for a profession.

Bill (second from right) and Joe (third from right) pose in 1952 with fellow animators (from left to right) Ed Barge, Irv Spence, Dick Bickenbach, and Ken Muse in a conspiratorial photo taken in Fred Quimby's office with all seven Oscars won for their *Tom and Jerry* cartoon series. *(Courtesy: Bill Hanna).*

With most major studios aiding the war effort by producing animated training films for drafted servicemen, MGM's Cartoon Department allotted much of its resources to create war-related instructional shorts, besides its usual program of theatrical shorts, to lift the spirits of millions of war-weary Americans. With the anti-Japanese fervor raging following the bombing of Pearl Harbor in December 1941 and the outbreak of World War II, Bill and Joe got into the act by directing a "pseudo-documentary" cartoon of their own, *War Dogs*. Released on October 9 of that year, the seven-minute Technicolor short follows the exploits of an army of infantry canines (the WOOFS) training for the war. That includes the film's mutt-like star, the incompetent Private Smiley. Asleep in his beige-colored tent (written above its opening, "Keep

Tom and Jerry in the holiday spirit as featured on the *MGM Club Studio News* in December 1946.

'Em Barking"), the four-legged sad sack dreams of heroically catching a Japanese soldier, but in reality is no hero. Typical of most animated fare of this time, the short features topical references to Hitler and war bonds and stereotypical Japanese caricatures that are deemed offensive today.

During the early 1940s, Bill and Joe tinkered with Tom and Jerry's physical appearance. They made Tom a more likeable bully and less mean-looking, giving him a more groomed, much smoother design and less detail for their unit animators to animate, with his famous shaggy fur, facial wrinkles, and overexaggerated eyebrows becoming more streamlined by end of the decade, and his overall appearance becoming taller and slimmer, more adult-looking, and more like a normal cat. Jerry, in contrast, physically changed the least. Only his ears were made slightly bigger, but he showed a greater range of emotion from "mischievous glee to cocky pride" and a more compassionate and good-natured side, and both characters, despite their inherent antagonistic nature, needing and caring for each other at times as the series went on.

By the mid-1940s, Bill and Joe's *Tom and Jerry* cartoons hit their stride. Their films moved at a much faster pace. Gags did not take as long to build. They just zipped off the screen as fast as they were developed. Their comedy style not only became more accelerated but also more violent. Working under the same roof with Tex Avery, Bill and Joe were influenced by Avery's more rapid-fire and energetic style of humor—from similarities in jokes to character reactions including over-the-top double takes and extreme slapstick humor—that would become standard traits of Tom and Jerry.

Despite such variations, the theme of each cartoon remained the same—cat chases mouse—only putting a different spin on the story each time out. In many respects, their Avery-influenced *Tom and Jerry* cartoons were more inventive and more outlandish than some of their predecessors. Often it became a race between cartoon units—Bill and Joe's and Avery's—as to which could produce the fastest cartoon. As Avery animator Michael Lah noted, "Each picture that would come out, from one unit or another, was faster. Pretty soon you got to the point where the only guys who could understand it were the guys who had worked on it."

Bill and Joe's growing importance to MGM only became more evident as their *Tom and Jerry* series climbed to the top of moneymaking short subjects in the industry. In 1944, their stature was enhanced when they won their second Oscar, for *Mouse Trouble*. Released to theaters in mid-November, Tom, up to his usual tricks, decides he must secure some outside help if he's ever going to succeed in catching Jerry. Therefore, he picks up a copy of a fabulous do-it-all book, *How to Catch a Mouse*, which offers some unorthodox methods of attack and capture that Tom can put into practice. It appears, after a series of mishaps, that Jerry must have read the book's counterpart, *How to Stop a Cat*, since he manages to escape every time and causes more harm to Tom than the book was worth.

The following year, they claimed their third Oscar—and fifth nomination—in a row for *Quiet Please!* (spelled with an exclamation mark in its opening title, unlike the studio's theatrical poster). Showing in theaters on December 22, 1945, Tom and Jerry's antics awaken the family bulldog, Butch. In order to resume the chase, Tom feeds the dog knockout drops and continues to battle Jerry until the canine recovers and puts a stop to it.

Despite the ongoing success of their *Tom and Jerry* series, one oft-stated criticism of Bill and Joe's films that emerged—repeated many times over throughout their careers—was that they were too violent. As Michael Barrier wrote in his article, "Of Mice, Rabbits, Ducks and Men: The Hollywood Cartoon": "Their characters suffered severe personal damage; tongues were cut off, teeth shattered. There was a gulf between the gags and the realistic style of the animation, and it could be filled with pain. The accusations of sadism or excessive violence . . . is, unhappily, appropriate for many of the Hanna-Barberas."

DANCING TO A NEW TOON

Regardless of such criticism, Tom and Jerry attracted attention far and wide and from the least obvious places. Studio star Gene Kelly wanted to feature Jerry in a dance segment that would combine animation with live action, something that had never been attempted, for his upcoming MGM feature directed by George Sidney, *Anchors Aweigh*. He approached Walt Disney about animating the dance scene of Jerry and him, but Disney declined, saying he was "too busy."

A scene from the live-action/animated segment of Jerry the Mouse and a sailor-suited Gene Kelly dancing together in the MGM musical, *Anchors Aweigh* (1945). © *Metro-Goldwyn-Mayer Inc.*

One morning in 1943, the determined 32-year-old actor approached Bill and Joe with his unique idea. "Gotta way to make your little Jerry mouse into a star," he said with a grin.

Kelly declared, "I mean a bigger star alongside of me."

Bill and Joe were both taken aback by his comment until Bill chimed, "But he is already a star, Gene."

Kelly had pleaded with Quimby to let him them do the scene using Jerry. The executive, not wanting to undermine MGM's dependably lucrative cartoon short series and commit a crew to work on such a technically challenging project, turned him down flat. Afterward, the tenacious actor used his good charm on Bill and Joe. Though enthusiastic, they told Kelly the decision was entirely up to Quimby. He took his pleas to studio president Louis B. Mayer, who crustily asked, after hearing his proposal, "Bill and Joe who?"

Kelly, a top studio star with formidable clout, convinced the curmudgeonly Mayer to approve the idea. Quimby then assigned Bill and Joe and the necessary resources to animate the sequence.

Entailing many hours and two intensive months to complete, Bill and Joe painstakingly animated the scene of Jerry matching step-for-step live footage of Kelly (who devised the dance himself) dancing with him. They took footage of Kelly and Rotoscoped it—a technique whereby animators trace each frame onto paper, to create a "blueprint" used to synchronize Jerry's movements with Kelly's in each frame. After shooting Jerry's performance against a blue matte background, both pieces—Kelly in live action and Jerry in animation—were composited to create the illusion of the sailor-suited actor and little monarch mouse gliding and dancing across the floor in perfect synchronization. Jerry—speaking one of the few times on camera—says, "I'm dancing!" While MGM produced a publicity still of Tom and Jerry dancing with Kelly, only Jerry actually danced in the film; Tom makes a cameo appearance as Jerry's valet.

Premiering on July 14, 1945, in movie houses nationwide, audiences went crazy over the sequence, with King Jerry's dancing with Kelly stealing the show and becoming one of the most remembered dance segments in MGM musical history. A year later, Sidney, impressed by the results, contracted them to create an animated sequence for the opening credits for his 1946 feature, *Holiday in Mexico*.

As 1946 approached, studios grew uneasy about the future of cartoons and feature films. Waiting in the wings was a new threat—television. That year, Bill and Joe tempered any doubts. They won over audiences after unveiling their newest recurring character in their latest *Tom and Jerry* cartoon, *The Milky Waif*: a syrupy sweet, inquisitive gray mouse with a large appetite as a coconspirator to Jerry and source of exasperation for Tom, Nibbles. The pint-sized troublemaker would costar

Theatrical movie poster from Bill and Joe's fourth Academy Award-honored Tom and Jerry cartoon, *The Cat Concerto* (1947). © *Metro-Goldwyn-Mayer Inc.*

in five more *Tom and Jerry* one-reelers, two of them Academy Award winners, *The Little Orphan* (1949) and *The Two Mousekeeters* (1952).

More importantly, Bill and Joe continued their string of consecutive Oscar wins, capturing their fourth statuette for their 29th *Tom and Jerry* short, *The Cat Concerto.* Produced in 1946 and first screened in theaters on April 26, 1947, their latest offering featured Tom as a tuxedo-clad concert pianist whose specialty is a rendition of Franz Liszt's *Hungarian Rhapsody No. 2* and whose dazzling keyboard techniques thrill concertgoers. Tom's playing also awakens Jerry, fast asleep inside the piano, jostling him around as the piano keys move. A reviewer for the *Motion Picture Herald,* a major Hollywood trade paper, hailed the one-reel subject, with comedy more subtle than their previous slapstick films, as "packed with amusing situations which will appeal to children and adults alike and it makes most of the skilled animation in unfolding the humorous story."

Controversy erupted on March 20, 1947, however, after the pair beat out a similar cartoon—using nearly identical gags and music by Liszt—to claim an Oscar over Warner Brothers' *Rhapsody in Rivets* at the 19th Academy Awards at the Shrine Civic Auditorium in Los Angeles. The film's director Friz Freleng implied that Bill and Joe took his idea, each accusing the other of plagiarism, after their cartoons were screened at that year's awards ceremony.

In mid-June 1947, Bill and Joe unleashed on audiences more inspired acts of cartooned madness with their 30th *Tom and Jerry* short, *Dr. Jekyll and Mr. Mouse,* seven minutes of diabolical fun with Tom transforming into a Jekyll-like character after downing a strange potion to terrorize his pee-wee sized friend, and Jerry then turning the tables on him by drinking a dubious mixture that turns him into a strongman "super rodent" to chase and squash his longtime adversary. The riotous adventure earned them their seventh Oscar nomination overall, but as original it was, it lost to director Freleng for his Warner Bros. cartoon *Tweetie Pie,* starring the precocious cat-and-mouse pair, Tweety and Sylvester, equaling the score between them.

The following year, Bill and Joe reclaimed the crown by garnering their fifth Oscar for *The Little Orphan.* Produced in 1948 and qualified for Oscar consideration after a one-day run in Los Angeles later that year,

Poster advertisement for Bill and Joe's sixth Oscar-winning Tom and Jerry cartoon, the swashbuckling send-up, *The Two Mouseketeers* (1952). © *Metro-Goldwyn-Mayer*.

the short was actually released a whole year later on April 30, 1949. It centers on the appetite of a baby mouse that, with Jerry's aid, helps itself to a bountiful Thanksgiving dinner. When Tom intervenes, the utensils on the table become deadly weapons which rout the enemy. The cartoon short has "everything a cartoon should have and a little more than some other 'greats' in the field," wrote a critic for *Box Office* magazine.

Not only did Bill and Joe walk off with an Oscar in 1948, but their next *Tom and Jerry* film, released immediately after *The Little Orphan* in May 1949, *Hatch Up Your Troubles*, also earned them their eighth Oscar nomination, losing to Chuck Jones's *For Scent-imental Reasons*. The hilarious cartoon short shows the more protective nature of Jerry, who ends up playing mother to a baby woodpecker that falls from the nest in a tree (after his real mother posts a sign, "Gone to Lunch. Back in 10 Minutes") and hatches in Jerry's bed, becoming easy prey for the tabby cat who plans to swallow him for dinner.

By the late 1940s, with movie theaters struggling to turn profits, the longevity of cartoon shorts again came into question. The decline had begun in 1948, after the Supreme Court declared the practice of block-booking, whereby theater owners were required to buy short subjects "sight unseen" to book with major feature films, as "an illegal, unfair trade practice." The ruling severed a stable revenue stream that studio's needed to bankroll their films, including short subjects. With television undermining their existence, theaters began double-booking features and eliminating screenings of cartoons in some cases. This meant less of a return on the dollar for cartoons and other short subjects affected by the change. As one industry official said, "There just wasn't any money left in cartoons."

Cartoons and live-action comedy shorts endured for the short term, including *Tom and Jerry*, with Bill and Joe adding two more cinematic triumphs to their long list of accomplishments. On April 7, 1951, movie-goers were treated to more rollicking fun in *Jerry's Cousin*. The Technicolor one-reeler—and 57th overall—puts Tom right in the middle of trouble that he is not expecting when Jerry's street-mean, strongman cousin, Mus-cles, shows up. He makes mincemeat out of the feisty suburban house cat who finally shoos the miniature menace out of sight with the help of his alley cat friends. In this classic battle of brawn and brains, Muscles triumphs, with Tom relenting to his superior strength. Initially developed under two working titles, *City Cousin* and *Muscles Mouse*, the film—actually made in 1950 but released nationally a year later—was no match for a newcomer to the scene: United Productions of America's (UPA) *Gerald McBoing-Boing*, which took home the Oscar in the best short-subject category in 1950, the year both films were nominated.

In 1951, Bill and Joe won their sixth Oscar for their 65th *Tom and Jerry* short released the following March, *The Two Mouseketeers*. Set in 17th-century France, Jerry the mouse and his screen companion Nibbles (voiced by Francoise Brun-Cottan), are the king's musketeers. When Jerry and his fellow musketeer arrive at the palace, they notice a huge table garnished with food, which is guarded by Tom. When the starving mice attack the table, Tom puts up a game fight to protect the food. As one movie critic wrote: "Only one fault could possibly be found with this cartoon. It's not long enough."

CHANGING DIRECTIONS

In mid-December 1952, Bill and Joe traveled to England to work on a fantasy cartoon sequence with actor Gene Kelly for his original all-dance musical anthology feature, marking his directorial debut, *Invitation to Dance*. The famous song-and-dance man directed, choreographed, and starred in the film, which was told as three stories entirely set to music and intricate dance moves without dialogue: "Circus," a classical ballet; "Ring Around the Rosy," a second, modern ballet based on Schnitzler's play *Reigen*; and "Sinbad the Sailor," a third, modern dance version adapted from both classic children's fairy tales "Aladdin" and "Sinbad the Sailor," with Kelly dancing and mingling with cartoon characters in this musical fantasy.

That same week, Edwin Schallert of the *Los Angeles Times* reported from unofficial sources that "a feature-length Tom and Jerry cartoon" was in the works. The movie under consideration was to involve "Robin Hood type characters, with Tom and Jerry as valiant allies." Whether or not such a production was in development, four years later, Bill and

Joe directed their Robin Hood parody as a *Tom and Jerry* short instead, *Robin Hoodwinked*.

For *Invitation to Dance*, Bill and Joe had to create an entire mystical animated world, much more demanding in terms of production than their previous efforts, in which the action took place. This entailed creating lush cartoon backgrounds and an array of characters, everything from ornately turbaned palace guards to a giant serpent, choreographed with Kelly's every move as he blissfully waltzes with a bejeweled harem girl with whom he becomes smitten. As Joe stated, "This involved far more than getting a mouse to dance with a man."

Completing the film that year, MGM delayed its release over concerns about its "commercial viability" and marketing Kelly's experimental musical anthology to movie audiences. Opening in theaters four years later, on May 22, 1956, the live-action/animated feature was a financial flop but is highly regarded today as a landmark all-dance film.

Meanwhile, in 1953, Bill and Joe created another live-action/animated sequence, becoming another milestone achievement in their storied careers, for the MGM feature *Dangerous When Wet*, costarring Esther Williams and Latin screen star Fernando Lamas. This time, they developed a beautifully timed and choreographed dream musical sequence at a cost of $50,000. In the sequence, the athletic, swim-suited Williams playfully swims underwater with Tom and Jerry sporting swim flippers, with animated pink bubbles coming out of her mouth.

Although he never grew tired of doing cat-and-mouse cartoons, Joe had always dreamed of doing bigger things with his life. One of them, since seeing his first Broadway musical in high school, was writing his own play, a romantic comedy, *The Two Faces of Janus*. Though nothing materialized of that idea, while producing a series of comic books with a woman writer who had contributed material, Bea Sparks, Joe teamed up with her to write a second play. First called *Down to Earth*, he retitled it *The Maid and the Martian*. RKO optioned the property for $25,000, but the deal had "one minor catch:" Howard Hughes, who owned RKO, had to initial all deals. It was up to Joe and his agent to get Hughes to sign off on the deal.

Tom and Jerry swim side-by-side with MGM star Esther Williams in a live-action/animated dream sequence from the movie musical, *Dangerous When Wet* (1953). © *Metro-Goldwyn-Mayer Inc.*

The deal fell through. Production finally moved forward, though, after Gordon Hunt, then working with Bill and Joe at MGM and associated with a small theater, the Gallery Stage, read and produced the play in five days after another production they had scheduled fell through. In October, it opened to a packed house and rave reviews, with the *Los Angeles Herald-Express* calling it "a hilarious two hours."

Fred Quimby, who read about Joe's hit play in local newspapers, was confrontational. He raged, "You have a full-time job here."

Joe, then earning nearly $600 a week, seriously contemplated quitting and becoming a full-time playwright. After friends warned him, "You'll starve. Do you know what playwrights do? They starve," he smartly stayed put. Outside a few offers, including one by Ingo Preminger, the younger brother of director Otto Preminger and whose claim to fame was later producing the successful 1970 film *M*A*S*H,* to adapt his play into a film version, Broadway called and nothing more came of his play.

Although many fans consider *The Two Mouseketeers* Tom and Jerry's all-time best, others prefer Bill and Joe's seventh and final Academy Award-winner, *Johann Mouse.* Narrated by Hans Conried, the 75th series entry, opening in theaters on March 21, 1953, details the exploits of Tom, a would-be Vienna pianist whose master is Johann Strauss (whose work also inspired the film). More of a showcase of classical music than comedy, a critic for *Box Office* magazine remarked: "The delightful and original idea and the slightly accented narration have rarely been equaled in the short [subject] field."

In 1954, Bill and Joe recast Jerry's little impish companion, Nibbles, last seen in *The Two Mouseketeers,* as the French-accented, moonfaced mouse, Tuffy, in the follow-up and prequel, *Touché, Pussy Cat!* Nominated for their 13th Oscar, the short, released that December, picked up where its predecessor left off, this time with the malicious mouse costar as a Mouseketeer-in-training under Jerry's watchful tutelage who earns the coveted title after rescuing Jerry from Tom in dramatic fashion. The seven-minute short, though rich in humor and memorable overall, lost at that year's annual Academy Awards to director Stephen Bosustow's *When Magoo Flew,* starring the myopic Mister Magoo, for UPA.

The success of *Touché, Pussy Cat!*—the studio's first *Tom and Jerry* cartoon produced in CinemaScope—spawned two more *Mouseketeer* adventures, *Tom and Chérie* in 1955 and *Royal Cat Nap* in 1957, but released in 1958. From late 1954 to 1955, some *Tom and Jerry* films were simultaneously produced in both the standard format and widescreen CinemaScope.

Later that year, Quimby permitted Bill and Joe to produce a serious cartoon, one that would "leave audiences thinking," as Joe said. An

Bill (left) cowers as Joe uses a makeshift bow-and-arrow as they demonstrate a scene for producer Fred Quimby (center) for their upcoming Tom and Jerry cartoon, *Two Little Indians* (1953). © *Metro-Goldwyn-Mayer Inc.*

almost scene-for-scene remake of Hugh Harman's 1939 short *Peace on Earth*, with a slightly different story, titled *Good Will to Men*. Released on December 23, 1955, this longer-than-average one-reeler—approximately eight minutes and 27 seconds long—is a chilling story about the destruction of the human race by the H-bomb, as told through the eyes of an elder mouse and his group of choir-singing young mice practicing their version of "Hark! The Herald Angels Sing" for that week's service. Bill and Joe hoped this CinemaScope cartoon would make a statement that would stick in everybody's minds. It won several honors, including their 14th Oscar nomination that year and a *Parents Magazine* medal, but did not go over well with audiences. "No pun intended," Bill said, "It was a real bomb."

TAKING ON DUAL ROLES

With the average cost of a *Tom and Jerry* cartoon rising to $40,000, Quimby, who had been steering MGM's Cartoon Department since its formation, retired that year because of ill health. Consequently, Bill and Joe were elevated to run the department and serve in dual roles as producers and directors of all remaining MGM cartoons, including Tex Avery's *Droopy* series (helmed after his departure by Michael Lah) through 1957. Some cartoons were released a year after the studio was shut down, including Bill and Joe's 15th Oscar-nominated short overall and first as producers, *One Droopy Knight*, that Lah directed.

Facing harsh economic realities and reduced budgets due to the falling box-office revenue, hoping to turn a profit, Bill and Joe doubled production, producing all of MGM's remaining animated films in widescreen CinemaScope and in limited animation using fewer cels per second. Their final batch of Tom and Jerry films—ones like *Busy Buddies*, *Tot Watchers*, and *Royal Cat Nap*—were not as imaginative as their earlier efforts. Animation was sleeker and linear, with characters looking more like cardboard cutouts and much more limited in their movements and stories that gave them no new comic terrain to explore.

Besides employing this much less expensive animation process, the addition of new animators to the staff may have affected the quality of these cartoons. Many, like Lewis Marshall and Ken Southworth, had never drawn Tom and Jerry. Unlike earlier animated favorites, there was a thicker ink line around the body of the characters as well. It made creatures like Jerry look fatter and distorted the overall appearance of other time-honored characters, including Tex Avery's Droopy.

As a last-ditch effort, Bill and Joe put a new spin on something old to entertain audiences. In 1957, they revived their popular father-and-son dog team, *Spike and Tyke*, supporting characters from their long-running *Tom and Jerry* series, to star in their own short-lived series of theatrical shorts. The characters first starring vehicle that year was the CinemaScope release, *Give and Tyke*. Tyke first appeared as a small-fry version with his ferocious-looking father—then named "Pup"—in the 1949 *Tom and Jerry* cartoon *Love That Pup*. Four years later, they were officially called Spike and Tyke starting with the *Tom and Jerry* short *That's My Pup*, stirring up trouble in four more cat-and-mouse cartoons before they were cast in their own series.

Both producing and directing took a terrible toll on Joe's personal life. While he worked many long hours, Dorothy was left all day to raise their three children, Lynn, Jayne, and Neal, by herself. As a result, as he wrote, "Dinners at our house were not the Ward-and-June-Cleaver love feasts," with Dorothy usually stepping outside, leaving Joe to "argue with my offspring about finishing their food and drinking all their milk."

Joe's home life was not "as dire" as he admitted. Unlike his own father who ranted, raved and was heavy-handed, he was a loving father who delighted in telling his children stories and creating Tom and Jerry drawings for their friends, some done on paper napkins at birthday parties. One famous original tale he described was "a never-ending bed-time serial" involving a cowboy character called Billy, dreaming up new adventures on the spot as he put his kids to bed. As things turned out, his children all ended up loving the cartoon business and later working in the studio—Lynn as a freelance colorist, Jayne as a senior vice president of Hanna-Barbera for 28 years, and Neal as a story man and story editor (his first story credit: 1967's *Birdman and Galaxy Trio*) before becoming a successful screenwriter and producer.

By slashing costs, Bill and Joe had hoped to keep the MGM cartoon unit operating. That never happened. Revenues kept sliding—due to slumping box-office sales and low rentals—with studios taking two years to recoup their costs for producing a single cartoon. Despite their best efforts and, in Joe's opinion, their *Tom and Jerry* cartoon showing "no signs of flagging," MGM's Cartoon Department was languishing in "red ink." The CinemaScope cartoons were not drawing and limited animation had not saved as much money as they had predicted. After Arthur Loew Sr., president of MGM, reviewed the books, he concluded the studio would reap a 90 percent profit by simply rereleasing the old *Tom and Jerry* cartoons instead of producing new ones. Thus, he phoned Bill and Joe's business manager instead of speaking to them directly, and their business manager then conveyed the bad news to them second-hand: "Close the studio. Lay everybody off." As Joe explained, "Twenty years of work suddenly ended with a single phone call!"

While accused of simply wanting to keep their jobs, Bill and Joe urged MGM to let them produce low-cost cartoons for television, but their proposal was rejected. MGM vice president Eddie Mannix simply believed there was no future in cartoons made for television. As Joe recalled, "Hollywood was under siege by a one-eyed box that had not only pushed radio out of the living room, but that was keeping people on their sofas and out of the movie theaters."

Whatever the case, the studio's Cartoon Department came to an unexpected end as did Bill and Joe's careers—with Joe equating its demise to "the fall of the Roman Empire"—where they had made a huge mark. (Several attempts were made to revive the *Tom and Jerry* series in the early 1960s, with Gene Deitch and Chuck Jones producing.) Surprised, Bill and Joe never thought the studio would permanently shut them down. After all, it had produced 313 theatrical cartoon shorts, that were recipients of 21 Academy Award nominations, including 10 Oscars.

After completing work on their final theatrical MGM *Tom and Jerry* short, *Tot Watchers*, released a year after their departure, Bill and Joe, deeming themselves a "hot commodity," shepherded their services from one studio and agency to another in hopes of finding new positions. With no takers, they found themselves at a major crossroads, neither eager to learn a new trade, until an idea struck them, one that would forever transform the same medium that had threatened their livelihood.

Blazing a New Path

Walking out of the MGM studio on their last day, Bill and Joe were at a loss over what their future would hold. As Joe later confided, "You have to realize that two guys who worked for twenty years on Tom and Jerry and had won every award, including seven Oscars, could not understand why the phone rang and a voice said, 'Close the studio.' There was no warning. It was just close the studio. We were the best in the business and what were we going to do now. Sell hamburgers?"

Less than four weeks after being discharged, the famous cartoon pair did better than that. Setting up their own home-based studios, they went to work. Then, mortgaging their futures, they pooled an initial investment of $30,000 (leaving them both "lunch money for about a month," Bill said) and formed their own animation company, H-B Enterprises.

On July 7, two months after MGM closed its animation studio, they rented offices at famed movie comedian Charlie Chaplin's old studio, now named Kling Studios, at 1416 N. La Brea Avenue in Hollywood, as their temporary home. Appointing iconic MGM director George Sidney, who had offered to serve as their business partner, as company president, they intended to produce cartoons for television. It was a great risk considering animation was "the poor stepchild of the television boom" and original animation was almost unheard of. As Joe stated to a reporter, ". . . we thought about TV. Where else could we go? We figured it was possible kids might get tired of old guys in clown outfits being real friendly, and then turning on old, old cartoons."

Neither was new to this thriving medium. While Bill and Joe were still churning out *Tom and Jerry* cartoons for MGM, a friend of Joe's at an advertising agency doing an ad campaign for Pall Mall cigarettes approached them about doing animated commercials for one of his clients. Working on the side under a shroud of secrecy, they anonymously produced with animator Gene Hazelton three or four animated spots for CBS television's popular sitcom, *I Love Lucy*, starring Lucille Ball and Desi Arnaz. Shortly thereafter, L. K. Sidney, one of the "Big Three" at MGM, quietly enlisted them to produce two one-minute animated commercials for television to promote two of the studio's upcoming features, *Scaramouche* (1952), a French Revolution drama, and *Pat and Mike* (1952), a five-time Academy Award-nominated romantic comedy costarring screen legends Spencer Tracy and Katharine Hepburn.

Before retiring, their old boss, Fred Quimby, unaware of their clandestine television work, actually called them into this office one day and suggested: "If you fellas really want to see how to handle TV for advertising, you should take a good look at the promos for 'I Love Lucy.' *That's* the way this thing should be done!"

With the market for theatrical cartoon shorts "virtually dead," the only choice they had to keep producing cartoons was to streamline the production side and costs. During their heyday at MGM, a single seven-minute *Tom and Jerry* cartoon in full animation required as many as 60 drawings per foot of film to produce. As Joe related, "The costs came from all the drawings—the hand work. We figured we could cut down on the animation by planning."

Still in its infancy, television executives had to settle for production costs that were far less than they could usually recoup within a year through advertising sales and revenue. Bill and Joe were by no means the first to usher in a more cost-effective style of animation

Bill (left) and Joe appear in an early promotional photo after forming their own cartoon studio, initially called Hanna-Barbera Enterprises. © *Hanna-Barbera Productions.*

on television; they were just the most successful. Outside of the first made-for-television cartoon series eight years earlier, *Crusader Rabbit*, television had become glutted with reruns of repackaged theatrical cartoons shown mostly as "filler" on adult-hosted kid shows on local independent television stations and in some form on major networks. "When we went into television," Joe remembered, "there was practically no original animation produced for the medium. We had to help test new methods of animating for TV. Television didn't have the money; it also didn't have the time."

From the start of their fledgling company—with Joe acting as pitch man and Bill supervising all production (a long-standing division of labor that remained throughout their television partnership)—they set out to give networks what the market would bear: cartoons made quickly and cheaply while making a profit. For their first production, they turned to characters that instead of being eternal antagonists were friends—a smart, clever cat and a big, dumb bulldog—in madcap outerspace adventures, called Ruff and Reddy.

After 17 years of doing "chase" cartoons with Tom and Jerry, neither were convinced that a slapstick approach would work well on small television screens. Instead they believed TV cartoons should be based on good stories with dialogue. Joe created the first *Ruff and Reddy* storyboard at his home, with his then-teenage daughter, Jayne, coloring the art for him. With his finished storyboard in hand, he and Bill pitched their concept to prospective distributors with little success. "We were turned down by MCA, ZIV, and 20th Century Fox, none of whom would see cartoon stories for television," Joe recalled.

BREAKING THROUGH—AT LAST

Down to their last hope, they met with a man who shared their vision: John H. Mitchell, vice president of sales for Screen Gems, Columbia Pictures's television distribution division. Mitchell was convinced animation could be readily produced for television and that there was a place for new and original animated anthologies, sitcoms, and variety shows. In fact, Screen Gems was already syndicating to 11 Western states a series of cheaply made, limited-animated cartoons airing on CBS-TV's *Captain Kangaroo*, called *Adventures of Pow Wow*, produced by an outfit called Tempe-Toons. Mitchell's idea, which he proposed to Columbia president Harry Cohn, was to produce new cartoons to bookend with Columbia's stockpile of old theatrical cartoon short subjects that were collecting dust. Fortune smiled down on Bill and Joe from the moment they walked into Mitchell's office. As Joe stated, ". . . we went to Screen Gems, put the storyboard on the floor, explained it and in fifteen minutes we had a deal."

Though the deal was consummated, getting what they wanted came after much cajoling on their part. Under the terms of the deal, Mitchell paid them a mere $2,700 per cartoon to start, contingent upon acceptance of their pilot film and "after great negotiating and pleading," Joe said. In return, Screen Gems would own 20 percent of their company, infusing them with the working capital to produce their series.

That fall, Mitchell commissioned them to produce a five-minute pilot. Using the animation technique they developed in doing their *Tom and Jerry* cartoons, Bill and Joe produced a pencil test of the first cartoon. They used only 1,500 colorless outline drawings (instead of the usual 25,000 to 40,000 drawings for a fully animated *Tom and Jerry* short) moving across the screen without sound or dialogue. "You had to be an animator to understand where to use those drawings," Joe explained, "and how to use camera moves to give it more life. We couldn't do the pantomime we had used in the *Tom and Jerry* series, because it took too many drawings."

When the shrewd and ruthless Harry Cohn saw the finished product, he immediately dismissed them and their idea: "Get rid of them! Just drop the whole idea!"

Their television career with Screen Gems seemed to be over before they had finished "a single cartoon."

Fate intervened in their favor. At the same time of Cohn's decision, NBC network executives had reviewed the same film and signed off on Mitchell's idea of coupling Bill and Joe's *Ruff and Reddy* cartoons with the studio's old cartoons. As Joe later wrote, however, it still took "all of John Mitchell's formidable powers of persuasion to talk Cohn into financing the creation of new cartoons for television." NBC, not yet ready to slot an all-half-hour cartoon show by itself on Saturday mornings, subsequently bridged Bill and Joe's new *Ruff and Reddy* and Screen Gems's Columbia Pictures cartoons with a currently live New York children's television show by *The Howdy Doody Show* producer Roger Muir. It starred a human host, Jimmy Blaine, and his stalwart cast of puppet characters: Rhubarb the Parrot and Jose the Toucan.

Bill and Joe hired many of their former MGM staffers, including animators Carlo Vinci, Kenneth Muse, Lewis Marshall, Michael Lah, Ed Barge, and layout artists Ed Benedict and Richard Bickenbach, to produce the first group of five-minute episodes. As a result, they imposed strict, new shooting standards and a more economical system of animation—in essence, a streamlined version of the way they created detailed pencil tests for their cartoons at MGM, using fewer drawings to complete a cartoon. Their stripped-to-the-bones system—that they called "planned animation"—thus would use fewer moving parts for the principal characters (without having to animate the rest of the body), reuse character walks or standard movements in cycles, and one background in an entire scene. The final cartoon was timed to its exact time length and produced much more rapidly, as a result. This established form was something they would use effectively for nearly three decades.

Later discussing this method they also used in *The Huckleberry Hound Show*, Joe said, "For instance, you want to show Huckleberry Hound about to go out on a chase, and you have him going into a closet putting on an overcoat, walking out. You can get the same effect by cutting from Huckleberry outside the closet talking to another character to Huckleberry in the closet with this coat on. Time-consuming drawing is cut in two."

Although both were old hands in the industry, others scoffed at the notion they could be successful with this new approach. One pro in the business reportedly put their odds of success at "a thousand to one," believing their idea was "too drastic." As Bill later admitted in an interview with the *New York Times*, "When we started the limited animation, it disturbed me. Then when I saw some of the old cartoons on TV,

I saw that actually, limited animation came off better on the dimly lit television screen than the old fully animated things."

Due to the tight budgets at the time, however, Bill and Joe realized they had little margin for error. As Joe confessed, "If we start making mistakes, we're in trouble because retakes are too expensive for TV."

In the end, Bill and Joe settled on a final concept they believed children would love, with the spaceship-bound feisty bow-tied Ruff and dimwitted Reddy, aided by the kindly pint-sized Professor Gizmo, foiling the plans of galactic villains, including Killer and Diller, the Terrible Texas Twins, Captain Greedy, Salt Water Daffy, Chickasaurus, and the Goon of Glocca Morra, in a crazy world. With such bare-minimum animation and less substance than more fully animated cartoons, they relied much more on vocal characterization and dialogue to succeed and engage younger viewers. Therefore, they chose two reliable mainstays from their latter days at MGM to voice their cat-and-dog tandem: Don Messick and Daws Butler. Messick's vocal characterization as Ruff was similar to his later squeaky-voiced impish mouse Pixie (of *Pixie and Dixie* fame), with Butler lending his tried-and-true Southern drawl as Reddy. They also voiced other characters, with Messick similarly serving as the narrator. In Bill and Joe's minds, they were the perfect combination—seasoned and skilled talent able to breathe life into their newly animated creations.

Although most animated cartoons shown on television were in black and white, Bill and Joe elected to produce the entire *Ruff and Reddy* series in color, even though it initially aired in black and white. They said to each other, "Color will be here soon on television. Cartoons last forever. Let's go ahead and do them in color, and we'll be a jump ahead of the game." As Bill later noted, "It was one of the smartest things we did."

Five short months later, however, Bill and Joe cracked the television market with barely a whimper. On December 14, 1957, emanating from WNBC-TV studios in New York and sponsored by General Foods Post Cereals, the low-cost *The Ruff and Reddy Show,* supplanting Art Clokey's clay-animated *Gumby* cartoon series, debuted on NBC directly after the highly rated *The Howdy Doody Show.* Its first season was not

Original model sheet from Bill and Joe's first made-for-television cartoon series, featuring the cat-and-dog duo, Ruff and Reddy, and costars (clockwise) Flipper, Professor Gizmo, Pinky, and Wooly the Sheep Dog, *The Ruff and Reddy Show.* © Hanna-Barbera Productions.

shown in every market, though, as many network affiliates preempted them in favor of their own programming. So the series did not fully take off until the spring of 1958, after more affiliates regularly aired it and it caught on with kids. Each half-hour telecast featured the likeable cat-and-dog duo in simplistically humored, serialized cliff-hanging wraparounds in 13 first-run adventures (two per show) in the style of

Crusader Rabbit, making up one complete story. They were bookended, showing before and after two old cartoon shorts from the Columbia Pictures film library, including the *Color Rhapsodies, Fox and the Crow,* and *Li'l Abner.*

Except for occasional glitches, Bill and Joe's execution of their new system of animation was nearly perfect. As Joe admitted in a 1958 interview, "We've left out an arm once in a frame, and a couple of times we may shoot with the wrong background, but, on the whole, technically, the shows are OK. I think the series is funnier and better than the Tom and Jerry shorts. The people who work with us think so, too. We can survive on TV and do it well."

Becoming a hit with young audiences, with Ruff becoming TV's first most famous original "talking cat," *The Ruff and Reddy Show* was broadcast for three seasons, the first two in black and white, until June 1959. That fall, the same year television went color, the program aired its third season entirely in color until the network replaced it the following October with *King Leonardo and His Short Subjects.* (In the spring of 1962, NBC revived the series with a new live host, Captain Bob Cottle, and cadre of puppets, Jasper, Gramps, and Mr. Answer, until its last broadcast on September 16, 1964.)

While *Ruff and Reddy* never achieved the superstardom of Bill and Joe's later characters, they did prove that limited animation and such mass-production techniques were feasible, low-cost ways of filling children's viewing hours. Employing a staff of only about 20 and farming out animation elsewhere, they practically worked seven days a week to produce *The Ruff and Reddy Show,* with others on the drawing board. Their success made other industry professionals take notice. As Bill noted at the time, "I think our cartoons are better than our fancy Tom and Jerry movies. We use close-ups, our shows are easier to watch, and we let the viewer use a little imagination."

MAKING HISTORY WITH A HOUND DOG

During *The Ruff and Reddy Show's* second season in 1958, Bill and Joe unveiled their first half-hour cartoon series made specifically for television: *The Huckleberry Hound Show*. Stripped for first-run syndication, the half-hour anthology series premiered on WPIX in New York on October 2, and aired weekday afternoons nationally just before primetime. The series starred the laconic, Southern-drawled, rubbery-faced, blue hound dog (also the show's emcee) singing off-key renditions of "Clementine" as he walked nonchalantly into disaster in at least one daily adventure. Wrapped around original episodes were two other components. The first was *Yogi Bear*, featuring Jellystone Park's incurable, picnic-basket-snatching bear (whose voice is reminiscent of Art Carney's Ed Norton from TV's *The Honeymooners*) and half-pint, bow-tied, bear cub pal, Boo Boo, who would prove to be the series' most popular character. Joe originally drew them as "two itinerant bears"—hobo bears—deciding from a list of 80 names, including Bumpkin Bear and, his first choice, Huckleberry Bear, before deciding on Yogi Bear, a deliberate reference to New York Yankees catcher Yogi Berra. The second segment was *Pixie and Dixie*, a delightful variation of Bill and Joe's cat-and-mouse-chase themes starring two mice—the blue-bow-tied Pixie and red-vested Dixie—who outfox and torment their tricky adversary, Mr. Jinks (spelled by Hanna-Barbera as Mr. Jinx but as "Jinks" in the film credits), the cat who hates "meeces to pieces."

Joe claimed in interviews during the series' successful first season run that he wrote the first 26 installments before turning it over to gifted former Warner Bros. cartoon story man and gag man Warren Foster at the start of the second season (his first episode being "Grim Pilgrim"). Bill and Joe had hired Foster, along with story man Michael Maltese, as their studio's new head writers. Charles Shows and Dan Gordon served as series writers during the first season, starting with the premiere episode, "Huckleberry Hound Meets Wee Willie."

The Huckleberry Hound Show also marked the arrival of the studio's new musical director, Hoyt Curtin, responsible for penning the show's catchy theme song and many other memorable themes for the studio's later hit cartoon series, including *The Quick Draw McGraw Show; The Magilla Gorilla Show; Wally Gator; Top Cat; Scooby-Doo, Where You Are You!; The Smurfs*; and others. For some shows, like *The Flintstones* and *The Jetsons*, he scored the themes right over the telephone. Bill and Joe phoned him and read him the lyrics, and then he would call back minutes later and sing a freshly written theme to them.

Huckleberry's creation resulted after the show's sponsor, Kellogg's, requested a new cartoon character. After an all-night sketching session, the character was spawned. Bill and Joe already had the name in mind and "liked the sound of it." Huckleberry's creation was a combination of Joe's recollections of Tex Avery's deadpan, droop-jowled basset hound, Droopy, and voice actor Daws Butler's array of Southern eruditions.

John Mitchell of Screen Gems actually sold *The Huckleberry Hound Show* over the phone to executives at Kellogg's. When they first proposed the character, however, one of its representatives objected over concerns that the name "Huckleberry Hound" was "a bit too long for a television screen." During his visit to

Conceptual drawing of Bill and Joe's laconic blue Southern hound dog, Huckleberry Hound, created at the urging of their sponsor Kellogg's. © *Hanna-Barbera Productions.*

Chicago to pitch the show to the Kellogg's people in concert with the Leo Burnett Agency, then representing the cereal company giant, Joe also presented another piece of footage. This featured a black-belted mouse character—smaller than Pixie and Dixie—to aid them in their ongoing battle with Mr. Jinks: Judo Jack. Speaking in a Marlon Brando dialect (as voiced by Butler), the Japanese karate mouse appeared in the second *Pixie and Dixie* cartoon made that year, "Judo Jack."

Critics praised *The Huckleberry Hound Show* as "a welcome addition" to weekday children's program lineups, with one Los Angeles critic "absolutely smitten" with the show's "Freshness in music, voices, dialogue and characters." Audiences identified with the hound's love of colloquial expressions and everyman status as an expert skier, big game hunter, bullfighter, and rescuer of damsels in distress who simply shrugged off his misfortunes in numerous exploits. The show became an instant hit. Following his first television appearance that October, *The Huckleberry Hound Show* attracted a higher interest among adults than Bill and Joe's predecessor, *The Ruff and Reddy Show.*

One reason for *Huckleberry Hound's* success was that "it's difficult to believe that Huck and his pals are cartoons." As *Los Angeles Times* writer Jean McMurphy noted at the time: "Perhaps the most unique thing about Huck and his crew is their dialogue. The drawings are excellent, the music is great, but the conversation is really in a class by itself."

Bill and Joe took their success in stride. As Joe stated then, "People seem to like our new characters and the simple backgrounds. We use top talent. Some of our people, now with a staff of 150, have been with us for 20 years. They are all tops in the field."

They operated under the belief that "children can understand a great deal more than adults realize." As a result, they did not write scripts that talked down on a child's level or that were afraid to use puns. Case in point: In one cartoon, after being punished for stealing a witch's broom and riding around on it pilfering picnic lunches, the Art Carney-like Yogi said: "They lowered the *broom* on me."

In running their studio, Bill and Joe had an "open-door policy" whereby their staff could come and see them about "anything, any time." As Joe added, "It's our way of keeping in touch with all phases of the operation." They were proud of their studio's informality and resentful of the word "factory" to describe their incessant output of television cartoons. As Joe once said, "We have no time clocks here. We have no closed doors and nobody makes appointments. They come in when they want, and they leave when they want. All they make is money—and cartoons."

By January 1959, Hanna-Barbera had already produced a stunning 170 cartoon episodes with its two series. *The Ruff and Reddy Show* and *Huckleberry Hound* aired during the dinner hour in 180 cities throughout the United States, and their technicians dubbed shows in Spanish and French for foreign markets. Their studio's high output and success proved, as Joe stated, "it's possible to make cartoons for profit on TV. No one else is doing it yet, but they will."

Huckleberry Hound and friends developed such an avid fan base—including adults—that on the night of May 9, 1959, when the program was preempted on CBS affiliates by an Edward R. Murrow interview, many viewers in Los Angeles complained. One woman ranted, "What happened to Huckleberry Hound? He wasn't on last night. They haven't taken him off the air, have they?"

Cecil Smith in his weekly *Los Angeles Times* television column encapsulated in a nutshell *Huckleberry Hound*'s widespread popularity this way:

> I asked my intellectual friend the other day over a dash of schnapps why Huckleberry enthralls him. His answer: "What makes Huckleberry Hound and his stock company so merry is that they don't labor their satire. Maybe they start for an agreed destination but in their half-hour progression they find so many opportunities to be absurd that they half-forget the main point and, like Aristophanes, lay about at everything. You can almost hate children enjoying Huckleberry so much; he is too good for the brats."

In a newspaper interview, Bill noted back then, "You know that Yogi and Huckleberry don't just belong to kids. Grownups know all about our animal friends."

While pee-wee viewers delighted in Huckleberry's antics and those of his famous costars, adults were right in step. In a survey of undergraduates, the *Yale Alumni Bulletin* reported that *Huckleberry Hound* was among the four top programs watched by Yale men. It became so frequently watched that seven scientists at the White Sands Proving

Grounds in New Mexico requested that an El Paso, Texas, station that aired the series in their area show it "at a later hour since they were too busy working on missile projects" during its normally scheduled time slot. A University of Washington fraternity similarly changed its dinner hour just so "they could see Huck," while servicemen on duty on the USS *Glacier* icebreaker in the Antarctica and the USS *Acme* minesweeper in the Pacific both named him as an honorary member of their crew.

True events often inspired their studio's cartoon lunacy. In the fall of 1959, Bill and Joe developed a story for an upcoming *Yogi Bear* cartoon premiering that October on *The Huckleberry Hound Show*. In the cartoon, titled *Rah Rah Bear*, Yogi attends a Chicago Bears–New York Giants pro football game to support the "bears" but is mistaken for their mascot. When the Bears organization heard of their plans, they were reportedly "delighted." As Bill recalled, "George Halas, coach and owner, said we could do anything we wanted." As Joe added, "We first got the idea when I saw a headline in late September on the sports pages. It went something like 'Giants to Clobber Bears.' I saw a football story with Yogi reading the headline and saying: 'Us bears have got to stick together.' So Yogi goes back and helps the burly bears win. It's kinda cute."

Soon after the high ratings success of *The Huckleberry Hound Show*, the character's popularity spread to requests pouring in for all over the country for the ubiquitous dog to make personal appearances at public events. Confronted with so many play dates and "without a body to deliver," Hanna-Barbera's distributor, Screen Gems, produced special human-sized Huck and later Yogi costumes. Costing several hundred dollars (later reported as $1,500) each, the costumes were sent by Air Express to outfit men hired in each city to climb inside and play the TV animal heroes at live appearances.

In September 1959, more fiery protests erupted after viewers were misinformed that *Huckleberry Hound* was "off the air permanently," inciting one reporter to quote Macbeth's famous rallying cry: "To arms." Actually, on September 28, the show had switched stations—from CBS affiliate KNXT Channel 2 to independent station KTTV Channel 11, with *The Huckleberry Hound Show* moving to the 6:30 to 7:00 P.M. (Pacific

Originally featured on *The Huckleberry Hound Show*, the picnic-basket stealing Yogi Bear and his accomplice Boo Boo were subsequently spun-off into their own half-hour series. © *Hanna-Barbera Productions.*

Standard Time) time slot. Placed in prime-time syndication nationwide to appeal to a larger adult audience, it was followed by the debut of Hanna-Barbera's second weekday series snapped up for the syndicated TV market: *The Quick Draw McGraw Show.*

"I'LL DO THE THINNIN' AROUND HERE, AND DOOOON'T YOU FORGET E-IT!"

Following the growing trend of Westerns being produced in Hollywood with no less than 29 television shoot-'em-ups airing in prime time, Bill and Joe developed their own satirical Western with an added twist. It starred a slow-talking, slow-moving, Stetson-wearing, sharp-shooting—and stupid—lawman and drawling mustang named Quick Draw McGraw ("And dooooon't you forget e-it!"). McGraw was joined by his diminutive Mexican burro deputy, Baba Looey, named after famed actor/singer Desi Arnaz's smash hit song, "Babalu," and whose rapid-fire Cuban cadence was patterned after Arnaz's. Together they corral every bad man of the prairie while meting out the Code of the West and poking fun at every Western cliché.

Serving as the show's host, the headstrong, upright, four-legged marshal, whose voice was patterned after comedian Red Skelton's famed Clem Kadiddlehopper character, also appeared in three six-minute cartoons. He scored huge laughs with audiences over his wacky antics to capture desperados. Occasionally donning a disguise as the fearless El Kabong (a takeoff of TV's *Zorro*), he carried out justice by smashing a guitar over the villain's head while rescuing a damsel in distress. He also enlisted the help of another supporting character to take down bad guys (first seen in 1959's *Bow-Wow Bandit*): a treat-loving bloodhound, Snuffles, whose begging for a powerful "Doggie Bis-kitt"—and when villains eat them, they turn into good guys—became a major hit with viewers.

Appearing opposite him during each 30-minute broadcast were two more recurring segments. *Snooper and Blabber*, cat-and-mouse private investigators and operators of the Super Snooper Detective Agency, rounded up criminals and tracked down missing animals in a parody of television detective shows like *Peter Gunn* and *77 Sunset Strip. Augie*

Doggie and Doggie Daddy featured canine father-and-son adventures with a long-suffering, Jimmy Durante-like father who is often the victim of his flowery, poetic son's ("Dear old bone-providing Dad") well-meant schemes. During the series' run, the *Snooper and Blabber* segments introduced another character who eventually starred in his own cartoons on *The Yogi Bear Show*: an overt Shakespearean lion with a Bert Lahr/*Wizard of Oz* Cowardly Lion voice called Snagglepuss (who also appeared under the name of Snaggletooth).

In reviewing Hanna-Barbera's latest conquest, one *Los Angeles Times* critic noted: "McGraw is actually designed for adult viewing although the animation pleases the children equally. But the dialogue is delivered with tongue in check. Only the big kids understand it fully."

Written by Michael Maltese and other top studio story men, *Quick Draw McGraw* was nominated for an Emmy Award, along with *The Huckleberry Hound Show*, for "Outstanding Achievement in the Field of Children's Programming." At the 12th Primetime Emmy Awards in June 1960, *Huckleberry* became the first cartoon show to win such an honor.

The Quick Draw McGraw Show remained in first-run syndication until September 1963. At that time the 45-episode series was repackaged and sold to CBS and added to its Saturday-morning lineup, where it became a permanent fixture for three seasons.

Hanna-Barbera's menagerie of animal characters became equally popular in another area: number-one in novelty sales around the country. Sales of licensed merchandise bearing the names and likenesses of Huckleberry Hound and Yogi Bear including comic books, records, and toy figures of every description, flooded the market. "The novelty business is astounding," Bill said at the time. "We can't keep up with it. It's all we can do to get our stories out on time. . . . We thought we could make a go of it on TV, but we didn't dream it would become this popular."

With their operation booming, in 1959, the newly renamed Hanna-Barbera Productions did an unprecedented $3.5 million in business as producers of television cartoons, succeeding with that rare combination of "good, well-timed, funny films" to meet the medium's growing

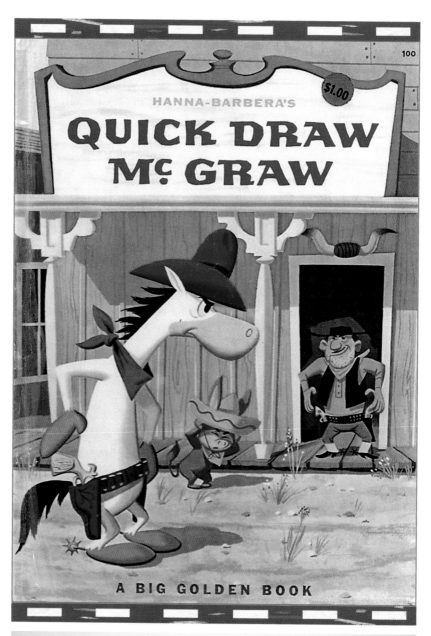

Full-color cover to the 1961 Big Golden Book based on Bill and Joe's character Quick Draw McGraw, published by Golden Books.

demand for original entertainment. With their "planned animation" supplanting the way cartoons were being produced, Joe stated, "Take the Disney method—the old movie method. It tried to mirror life. We don't. We spoof reality, but we don't mirror it. Our characters don't walk from a scene, they whiz. Movements that took 24 drawings under the old movie system take us four. We just keep the story moving."

With three half-hour cartoon shows on TV and a fourth coming, Bill and Joe signed a new five-year deal with Screen Gems. The deal also called for distributing through its parent company, Columbia Pictures, their first theatrical cartoon series, *Loopy De Loop*, the comical adventures of a charming French wolf using their same streamlined method of animation. Discussing the series, Joe told a reporter, "We've just made 12 cartoons in one month for theaters. Where we used to do eight a year at MGM, we now do 179 with approximately the same sized staff due to our new streamlined technique. Even Walt Disney hasn't been making many cartoons lately; lucky for us he slowed down as we were entering the field."

On November 5, Loopy De Loop was rolled out into theaters citywide in his first cartoon, *Wolf Hounded*. This so-called good Samaritan wolf opened each cartoon by saying, "I'm Loopy De Loop, the good wolf." He mangled the English language and was featured in comical exploits in which his unusually kind and helpful ways were not always welcomed by others because he was a wolf. Later repackaged for television syndication in the 1960s, Loopy appeared in 78 cartoon shorts, all released to theaters, until mid-June 1965.

Bill and Joe's entire MGM staff, who were much younger when they worked under the slower, more laborious method of full animation, had successfully switched to doing their new pared-down method despite many of them approaching middle age. "Our story men, Warren Foster and Mike Maltese, are all of 50 and they're fabulous," Joe noted. "No one ages in our business and these men have been cartooning since they were kids. Mike came to us from Warner's, and has a delicious sense of humor. He used to do eight theatrical cartoons a year, but wrote 78 stories for us in nine months—the entire *McGraw* series."

Hanna-Barbera's early success was due not only to its talented team of artisans and writers, but also to its main voice artists who became "voice kings" for the studio: Don Messick and Daws Butler. Butler provided the vocal characterizations of Huckleberry Hound, Yogi Bear, Dixie, Quick Draw McGraw, Snooper, Augie Doggie, and Doggie Daddy. Together they did "eight or nine voices, sometimes as many as seven in one cartoon" and often recorded voice tracks for four cartoons in one sitting.

While dominating television sets across the country with their original family-friendly cartoon fare, Bill and Joe's greatest challenge lay ahead: cracking prime-time television with a cartoon sitcom unlike any seen before.

6

Conquering Prime-time with America's Favorite Prehistoric Family

In 1959, proving conclusively their method of "planned animation" could succeed on television and be profitable, Joe and Bill's three weekday series, *The Huckleberry Hound Show*, *The Quick Draw McGraw Show*, and *Yogi Bear*, were flourishing on more than 100 television stations nationwide. Next, they heeded Screen Gems executive John Mitchell's call to develop a *true* animated cartoon show with continuing characters in half-hour escapades for prime-time.

In coming up with potential ideas, they considered hundreds of characters—drawing and reviewing them, fitting them in situations, and discarding those they did not like. Both longtime fans of CBS's classic sitcom *The Honeymooners*, starring comedian Jackie Gleason as the blustery bus driver Ralph Kramden, they liked a premise and characters mirroring the latter, with Joe sketching copious possibilities of their would-be stars, as Pilgrims, Indians, Romans, and others, in different settings. The idea that clicked with them looked back to the days when cavemen roamed the Earth. Studio artists Dan Gordon's and Ed

Benedict's preliminary conceptual drawings became the basis of what they ultimately created—a suburban Stone Age family comprised of a simple, ordinary caveman couple and their equally simple, ordinary caveman neighbors—known as *The Flintstones.*

Selling *The Flintstones* presented a formidable challenge. It represented a fresh concept—venturing beyond the usual six- or seven-minute cartoon format to a full half-hour animated sitcom in prime time no less. It was something that had never been attempted. As Joe stated, "It was a tough sell. At first we couldn't do anything right."

Joe spent two months trying to secure a sponsor. Embarking on whirlwind trips to Chicago, St. Louis, and finally New York, he appeared in dozens of boardrooms tacking up hundreds of storyboards to pitch the show, acting out all the roles in front of sponsors and ad agency people, and then "watching their eyes and their reactions, to see if they're smiling or if they're falling asleep."

In New York, Joe booked himself at the prestigious Sherry-Netherland, thinking he had to be there for a week. Instead, he remained long enough to "see the snow melt and the flowers come out" in Central Park with "My thumbs bleeding from all the thumb-tacking [of storyboards]." Both CBS and NBC turned it down as "too oddball, too risky." Just when he was about to give up, ABC, already planning to do creative counter-programming "bucking the trends" of the other networks, bought the series.

By that December, announcing plans for the tentatively titled *The Flagstones*, ABC purchased the rights for the unheard of sum of $80,000 per half-hour compared to $50,000 for live-action shows. Some Hollywood prognosticators reportedly "laughed in their martinis," predicting the "experiment" would result in a huge financial loss. Originally to air early in the 1960–1961 season, the series was renamed *The Gladstones* for a brief time after cartoonist Mort Walker complained the name sounded too similar to his suburban characters, The Flagstons, in his widely syndicated newspaper comic-strip, *Hi and Lois.*

By April 1960, Bill and Joe had retitled the show *The Flintstones*, and on May 1, ABC treated audiences to an advance network preview, still as *The Flagstones.* The one-minute and 42-second clip was of Fred

A scene from the one-minute and 42-second May 1960 pilot of *The Flintstones* aired on ABC, called *The Flagstones. (Courtesy: Cartoon Network).*

and Barney spear-fishing during lunch around a swimming pool (the scene was later used in the premiere episode, "The Swimming Pool"). For the pilot, Daws Butler provided the voices of both Fred and Barney, with June Foray as Betty; neither did the voices in the actual series. Veteran actor Alan Reed, best known for his role as the "poet" Falstaff Openshaw on comedian Fred Allen's radio program, and Mel Blanc were chosen as the voices of Fred and Barney, respectively, with Jean Vander Pyl and Bea Benadaret, remembered primarily for her television work on *The Burns and Allen Show* and *Petticoat Junction*, as Wilma and Betty.

Reed, known for his famous stentorian voice as Fred, actually came up with the character's memorable catchphrase. While recording one of the earliest episodes, after reading in the script the line called for him to shout, "Yahoo!," he asked Joe in the recording booth directing the session, "Hey Joe! Do you mind if I say 'Yabba-Dabba-Doo'?"

Joe simply shrugged and agreed. Afterward, the catch line stayed and Bill, liking the new phrase, added it to the lyrics of the show's theme song.

Neither Bill nor Joe limited their efforts solely to television animation. Director George Sidney was then a member of their studio's board after departing as president. Joe and Bill alternated annually in his place. Sidney contracted them to do animation work for his next live-action comedy feature, *Pepe* (1961), starring Mexican comedian Cantinflas. On February 10, 1960, the *Hollywood Reporter* reported that the famous cartoon pair was to create an animated "Don Quixote" dream sequence for the movie in which Cantinflas dreams he is Quixote "protecting his lady from harm." Two months later, columnist Hedda Hopper announced they were actually animating two sequences—another in which Cantiflas fights a bull. Though a studio synopsis dated March 21, 1960, discussed the *Don Quixote* sequence, neither scene made the final cut of the film, which was nominated that year for five Academy Awards.

In late June 1960, with their cartoon factory "spewing out drawings like spaghetti," as one writer described it, Bill and Joe announced plans to build their own studio within six months in North Hollywood. The new facility would be air-conditioned and include its own dining room. To accommodate their staff as it outgrew the former Chaplin studio, they rented offices converted into working studios throughout Hollywood and subcontracted equipment, a large capital outlay for a company that, as Bill said, was "still struggling to stay under the frugal production budgets."

Huckleberry Hound merchandise grossed an estimated $40 million that year, and by August, *The Huckleberry Hound Show* was viewed in prime-time syndication by an estimated 16 million Americans nightly on some 200 television stations. Kellogg's spent approximately $12 million on Hanna-Barbera's existing programs, which were also broadcast in Japan, Spain, France, England, New Zealand, Australia, and throughout Latin America.

GIVING BIRTH TO A TELEVISION CLASSIC

On September 30, 1960, Hanna-Barbera's "purely adult show" *The Flintstones*, sponsored by the R.J. Reynolds Tobacco Company and Miles Laboratories' "Once-a-Day Vitamins," took the airwaves. Previewed for critics, the imaginative half-hour series featured blowhard Fred Flintstone working as a gravel pit crane operator at the Rock Head & Quarry Cave Construction Company (their motto: "Feel Secure—Own Your Own Cave") in the small town of Bedrock. There he lived with his beautiful red-headed wife, Wilma, and their two pets, a dinosaur that barked like a puppy (Dino) and saber-toothed cat (Baby Puss), in their split-level cave. In the series opener, "The Flintstone Flyer," Fred and his giggling pal Barney Rubble go bowling on the same night their wives, Wilma and Betty, want to go to the opera after Barney purchases the tickets in advance. Although television audiences warmed up to the prehistoric cartoon show, critical reaction was mixed, perhaps resulting from higher-than-usual expectations. *Time* magazine praised television's newest sitcom parody, calling it a "first rate . . . approach to satire." *New York Times* critic Jack Gould, meanwhile, dismissed the show as "an inked disaster."

Bill and Joe actually wrote the script for the series' opener. But after realizing, as Bill said to Joe, "There's no way in the world that we can write all of these scripts," with Joe handling the recording of dialogue and Bill directing a new episode each week, they made Warren Foster head writer. For the next 15 weeks, he wrote one half-hour story per week and storyboarded each episode with Michael Maltese, also serving as one of its principal writers.

Production of *The Flintstones* was their most ambitious endeavor. The show required 43,000 individually exposed frames of film per half-hour, turning out more footage in two weeks than most cartoon studios did in a year. As with their previous programs, their latest achievement succeeded in using their pioneering "planned animation" technique: simple close-ups and short cuts reducing all speech to nine basic mouth movements while eliminating elaborate backgrounds. Bill intricately timed dialogue to match the action and exact number of drawings needed, and Joe also supervised the writing of each program.

Full cast photo of *The Flintstones*, including Fred (far left) and Wilma Flintstone, their pet dinosaur, Dino, and daughter, Pebbles, and Barney (far right) and Betty Rubble and their super-strong son, Bamm-Bamm. © *Hanna-Barbera Productions.*

Attracting 13,882,000 viewers, *The Flintstones* consistently destroyed all competition in its first season. It went on to receive an Emmy nomination and a Golden Globe Award for "Outstanding Achievement in International Television Cartoons." Then, by its second season, in 1962, the series beat such dramas as *Route 66* and *Detectives* in the ratings. Reviewers were much more enthusiastic. As *Variety* noted, "The satirical framework . . . seems plenty durable and of course it provides endless possibilities for sight gags."

Despite the series' first season success, Bill was the most critical. He told a reporter in January 1961: "I frankly told Joe that I was disappointed in the program and found it less imaginative than Huck Hound or Quick Draw McGraw."

Joe understood what his longtime partner meant. He told him, "You don't consider it 'adult.' But we never said it would be. That was all part of a publicity buildup. It was designed for early evening entertainment and the central characters are adults instead of animals. But nowhere in the format did we promise people an animated *New Yorker* magazine. We'd love to try it, but it would run about one week."

During a swing through New York that January visiting old friends at his former haunt, the American Institute for Banking, Joe, the chattier and more gregarious of the two, was proud of his and Bill's success overall. He hoped the current generation of American youngsters would someday view with the same fondness and nostalgia for Huckleberry Hound and Quick Draw McGraw his parents had reserved for Mickey Mouse and Donald Duck. "It may not be exactly my life," he stated with a smile, "but maybe it's my partner's."

As first reported on September 4, 1960, in the *Los Angeles Times*: "Yogi Bear not only is taking off from Huckleberry Hound for his own show but is also soon to star in a full-length movie . . . " On January 30, 1961, Bill and Joe scored an even bigger hit with their fourth half-hour syndicated series, *The Yogi Bear Show*. *Variety* hailed the series as "the funniest and most inspired of all the charming, contagious Bill Hanna–Joe Barbera characters . . . that he can be appreciated wholeheartedly by adults as well as children."

Yogi Bear was outgrowing his place on *The Huckleberry Hound Show*, spurring sales of licensed Yogi comic books, long-playing records, and toys. Bill and Joe originally wanted to introduce the blundering bruin in his own starring series in the fall of that year. However, that changed when Kellogg's jettisoned its sponsorship of UPA's *Mister Magoo* series in October 1960 and asked Bill and Joe to speed up production of a replacement. Three years since his *Huckleberry Hound* show debut, the scene-stealing bear had become Hanna-Barbera's biggest cartoon star. The new series starred the good-natured "Smarter than the average bear!" Yogi and his nasal-sounding sidekick Boo Boo in weekly adventures stealing picnic baskets from unwary tourists and eluding Jellystone National Park's rules-conscious Ranger John Smith (originally unnamed in 1958 episodes on the *Huckleberry*

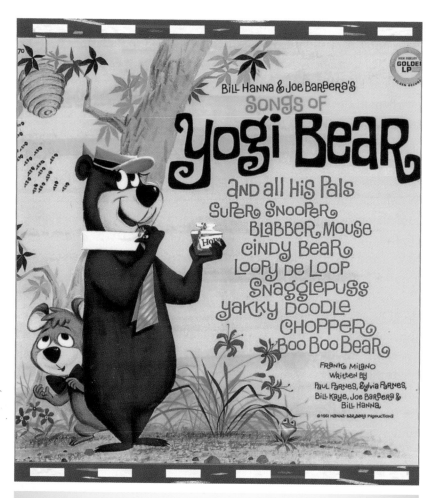

One of many popular Hanna-Barbera collectibles was this 1961 Golden Records album, *Songs of Yogi Bear and All His Pals.*

Hound series). The episodic cartoons also introduced a new character: Yogi's girlfriend, Cindy.

Sharing the spotlight were two new additions in six-minute adventures: *Snagglepuss*, the ultra-theatrical orange-furred lion ("Exit stage left!"), and *Yakky Doodle*, a mischievous pint-sized yellow-feathered duckling paired with a golden-hearted bulldog, Chopper, who protects the "little feller" from the duck-hungry Fibber Fox. Yakky, who first appeared nameless in a *Yogi Bear* cartoon in 1958, was reminiscent of Bill and Joe's diminutive duckling at MGM, Little Quacker. (Originally, according to media reports, the series was to introduce "a new actor, a crime-solving lawyer, Perry Gunite," as one of its components, but who instead appeared in the first season of *The Flintstones*.)

Becoming Hanna-Barbera's "goodwill ambassador," Yogi Bear generated an avalanche of national publicity that enhanced his onscreen persona and the stature of his creators. At the risk of oversaturation, Bill and Joe produced not only two seasons of new *Yogi Bear* cartoons but also a half-hour syndicated *Birthday Party* special, coproduced by Film-Fair, in 1963. They also reran earlier episodes on CBS's live-action Saturday-morning series *Magic Land of Allakazam*, and as part of a prime-time syndicated package a year earlier, pairing Huckleberry Hound and Yogi Bear for *The Best of Huck and Yogi*.

ENJOYING MORE HITS THAN MISSES

In the wake of the runaway success of *The Flintstones*, in 1961, television was inundated with four new prime-time series that fall: Jay Ward's *The Bullwinkle Show* on NBC and ABC's *Calvin and the Colonel, Alvin and the Chipmunks* (based on Ross Bagdasarian's celebrated hit song, "The Chipmunk Song"), and Hanna-Barbera's sixth cartoon show, *Top Cat*.

Before the start of the 1961-1962 season, the future of *The Flintstones* appeared in jeopardy after Mel Blanc, the voice of Barney Rubble, suffered a near-fatal automobile accident in January 1961. While driving his lightweight Aston-Martin sports car on a treacherous curve near UCLA, he crashed his car head-on into another and was not expected to live. During Blanc's prolonged hospitalization, Daws Butler filled in as the voice of Barney on five episodes starting with the first new episode of the second season that September, "The Hit Song Writers," recorded a month after Blanc's accident. Hal Smith, best known as Otis the drunk on TV's *The Andy Griffith Show*, also subbed as Barney in one episode until Blanc, bed-ridden in a body cast from his neck to his toes, was able to record his lines of dialogue from his bedroom at home. As

Joe recalled, "The easy thing would have been to replace him, but we kept going and it worked. Sometimes we'd have as many as 16 people crowded into his bedroom and we hung a mike in front of him."

With five shows on the air that season, including their three mainstays, *The Huckleberry Hound Show*, *The Quick Draw McGraw Show*, and *The Yogi Bear Show*, consistently ranking in the top 10 in every market, Bill and Joe produced a staggering 4,500 minutes of animation that season, more than any other studio. While some thought their studio's high output looked like overkill, they were unshaken by such criticism. They were devoted to providing worthwhile cartoon entertainment for children and adults. As Bill explained, "Children have introduced such characters as Huckleberry Hound and Yogi Bear to their parents. And now they all watch together. Once youngsters introduce a cartoon series to their elders, and if the show has any merit at all, the adults are hooked and become fans themselves."

On September 27, 1961, *Top Cat* debuted in its Wednesday 8:30–9:00 P.M. time slot. Facing stiffer competition, the animated ensemble series featured a conning bon vivant feline (affectionately called "T.C.") who led a gang of "hip" New York City alley cats—Fancy-Fancy, Spook, Benny the Ball, The Brain, and Choo-Choo. The show got off to a slow start. Even UPI entertainment writer Vernon Scott predicted the series had "good chance of having a can tied to its tail before the season is over." Cosponsored by Kellogg's and Bristol-Myers, the half-hour sitcom, inspired by the famous character Sgt. Bilko from *The Phil Silvers Show*, eventually attracted a devoted legion of viewers. By March 1962, it regularly topped CBS's detective series *Checkmate*, starring British star Sebastian Cabot, in its time slot. Despite its sudden surge, the 30-episode series lasted only one season, later finding new life in reruns on Saturday morning television.

In case *Top Cat* failed, Bill and Joe had three other cartoons waiting in the wings. *The Jetsons* was about a close-knit, middle-class, futuristic space-age family. *The Gruesomes* featured a prehistoric, Addams Family–like "family of sickniks"—Weirdly and Creepella, their son, Goblin, and uncle Ghastly—inspired by Hanna-Barbera's previous monster family, Mr. and Mrs. J. Evil Scientist. The third was a medley show of animal character-driven components: *Cops and Roberts, Bill and Coo*, and *Casey Bones*. *The Gruesomes* premiered a year later in a self-titled episode of *The Flintstones*.

Despite having one failure to their credit, Bill and Joe gambled again. Under the name of *The Hanna-Barbera New Cartoon Series*, they unleashed a collection of five-minute cartoons: *Lippy the Lion*, a wise-cracking lion, and his laughing hyena pal, Hardy Har Har; *Touché Turtle*, the swashbuckling exploits of a sword-wielding turtle and his sheepdog sidekick, Dum-Dum; and *Wally Gator*, an Ed Wynn-sounding (a legendary film and television comedian and voice in classic Disney animated films) alligator who escapes from a zoo. Television stations snapped up the show, and Screen Gems doubled its original order to 52 half-hour shows. On September 3, 1962, Bill and Joe's first made-for-syndication series not sponsored nationally by Kellogg's made its television debut, becoming yet another success for their studio. Much like their other creations, Hardy Har Har's (voiced by Mel Blanc) famous expression, "Oh gee, oh gosh, we can't do that!" became widely imitated by children.

Ten days later, on September 23, 1962, with America in the midst of a space race with the Soviet Union, ABC premiered Hanna-Barbera's space-age sitcom, *The Jetsons*. Set in the 21st century, the futuristic spoof revolved around George Jetson (voiced by George O'Hanlon), a computer digital index operator at Spacely's Space Age Sprockets who works for a grouchy boss, Mr. Spacely; his stay-at-home wife, Jane; his teenage daughter, Judy; his boy, Elroy; and their pet dog, Astro. Family adventures in their skypad apartment featured many technologically advanced gizmos, including their domesticated robot maid, Rosie. The 24-episode series was fresh, funny, homespun, and visionary, but ill placed. *The Jetsons* aired Sunday nights opposite two top-rated family shows: NBC's *Walt Disney's Wonderful World of Color* and CBS's *Dennis the Menace*. The show floundered despite original test audiences indicating it would become a bigger hit than *The Flintstones*. "When you have three family shows opposite each other, you're splitting your audience," Bill remembered. "We were perplexed and disappointed that it didn't do better in the ratings."

Bill (left) and Joe hold a chalk talk session drawing larger-than-life caricatures of themselves.

ABC subsequently cancelled *The Jetsons* after one season. Rebroadcast the following season on ABC's Saturday-morning schedule, the
show was received much more favorably by young viewers, as was *Top
Cat*, which ABC also moved that October to Saturday mornings.

Accelerating production at a frantic pace with their staff ballooning to 150 employees, Bill and Joe broke ground on much larger quarters in March 1962. The new location was a four-acre plot of vacant
land Bill had noticed—an area where he and his Boy Scout trooped
once camped when he was a kid. Designed by noted architect Arthur
Froelich, the $1.25 million California contemporary structure, located
at 3400 Caheunga Boulevard, featured an ultra-modern design with
a sculpted latticework exterior and lush offices, a moat, five beautiful
fountains, and a pine-tree-covered, park-like setting. While construction
took place, Hanna-Barbera temporarily occupied rented office space in

a building two blocks from the site. As Joe stated at the time, "This will be twice the size of our old building, a full two-story structure."

Worried that might be too small, the blue-eyed, wavy gray-haired Bill joked, "Maybe we should make it three stories."

Meanwhile, in early 1963, Joe's marriage to Dorothy ended in divorce. Shortly after they split, he met a bright, witty blonde at Hollywood's oldest eatery, the world-famous Musso & Frank Grill on Hollywood Boulevard. A bookkeeper and cashier by trade, Sheila Holden was the daughter of a British army colonel who came to America in 1960. Joe was attracted to her and made her his second wife. Unlike Dorothy, a stay-at-home mother who shunned Hollywood's social scene, Sheila was more Joe's match—a socialite at heart who frequented many gatherings with Joe. Five years later, they moved into a home perched high on a hill in Sherman Oaks, a San Fernando Valley suburb and a place they would call home for the next 26 years.

MAKING TELEVISION HISTORY

The February 22, 1963, episode of *The Flintstones* was the most anticipated television event since the birth ten years earlier of Little Ricky on CBS's *I Love Lucy*. The newest member of the Flintstone family made her debut: Fred and Wilma's long-lashed, red-haired daughter, Pebbles. Originally the baby was supposed to be a boy—a "chip off the old rock"—Fred Jr., but Joe changed it to a girl because Sheila, who knew the vice president of Ideal Toy, told him "We could have a hell of a deal [with Ideal Toy] if it had been a girl."

The off-screen birth in Bedrock's Rockapedic Hospital in the color episode, "The Blessed Event," was the high point of the series' third season. It began weeks earlier with a story arc of Wilma's pregnancy and continued with Fred and her adjusting to parenthood after Pebbles's birth. That fall, the Rubbles adopted a baby son left on their doorstep, who they named Bamm-Bamm.

After moving that year into their new location with 250 people under their employ (including both their daughters working as inkers and painters) and three more pilots in the works, Bill and Joe's most promising show bowed in first-run syndication that fall. *The Magilla Gorilla Show* starred its title character and also featured animated adventures of Punkin' Puss, Mushmouse, Ricochet Rabbit, and Droop-a-Long. Bill and Joe also planned to produce their first live-action comedy series and live-action films. One never got off the ground: *Father Was a Robot,* about a real-life New Mexico scientist, Dr. Iben Browning, building a futuristic robot that "can register pain and will react."

Entering its fourth season that fall, the popular caveman clan, *The Flintstones,* became equally famous in foreign markets. One promotional stunt was an electronic, larger-than-life, 300-pound Fred Flintstone able to speak in most languages that was sent to other countries. As Bill recalled in July 1963, "We sent it to Scandinavia, and 25,000 people were at the airport for its arrival. The tape recorder inside is turned on in whatever language we wish. He's now making his first appearance in Tokyo."

On June 3, 1964, Bill and Joe's long-awaited first feature, announced almost four years earlier, opened in theaters. *Hey There, It's Yogi Bear* (originally titled *Whistle Your Way Back Home*) was the first full-length animated cartoon based on a television program. In the 89-minute cartoon, Yogi and Boo Boo are sent packing by Ranger Smith—tired of Yogi's "pick-a-nick" basket stealing ways—to the San Diego Zoo. With a scant amount of animated theatrical films being produced, Bill and Joe were convinced the movie would create "a box office stampede." Praised by *Variety* as "artistically accomplished in all departments," with songs that were "pleasant, if not especially distinguished," the low-budget film was only mildly successful.

That fall, Bill and Joe redeemed themselves. Besides introducing the new, widely syndicated *Peter Potamus and His Magic Flying Balloon,* including two other components, *Breezly and Sneezly,* and *Yippee, Yappee, and Yahooey,* they introduced to audiences their first cartoon featuring realistic human figures using a new technique, called "animated illustration," *The Adventures of Jonny Quest.*

After seeing the 1962 James Bond spy thriller *Dr. No,* Joe was inspired to create the series after originally planning to produce a cartoon version of the popular radio serial *Jack Armstrong.* He produced a two-minute animated test sequence, hiring noted comic book artist

Sharing title with *The Flintstones* as Bill and Joe's most popular television creations since 1960 was the picnic-snatching Yogi Bear, so successful he was spun-off into the studio's first theatrical feature, *Hey There, It's Yogi Bear* (1964). © *Hanna-Barbera Productions.*

Doug Wildey to animate it. After negotiations to secure the *Armstrong* rights fell through, Joe retooled the idea as *Jonny Quest* (scenes from the Jack Armstrong test film are incorporated into the show's closing credits). Using Wildey's drawings and storyboards, Joe sold ABC and sponsors on the concept, originally titled *The Saga of Chip Baloo* and *Quest File 037*, selecting the character's name from a phone book. Young Jonny was partly inspired by film roles played by young actor Jackie Cooper and other works, including Milton Caniff's adventure comicstrip *Terry and the Pirates*, and Grosset & Dunlap's popular teen adventure book series *Rick Brant*.

Premiering on ABC on September 18, 1964, with the opening episode, "The Mystery of the Lizard Men," the high-tech action-adventure show became an immediate prime-time hit. The result was a series of fantastic adventures of the 11-year-old boy traveling the globe in search of adventure and intrigue with his scientist father, Dr. Benton Quest; Benton's 11-year-old, adopted, Indian son, Hadji; family bodyguard/ tutor, Roger "Race" Bannon; and their fearless black-masked bulldog, Bandit.

A departure from the usual television cartoon fare, *Jonny Quest* underscored their studio's ability to create a serious show in the action/ adventure format besides family-oriented cartoon sitcoms. Unlike previous incarnations whereby simple backgrounds were reused, the half-hour series was their most difficult production. They had never attempted to layout and draw new backgrounds, new locations, and new characters each week. "It takes four people to lay out 'The Flintstones,'" Bill recalled then, "and 30 to lay out *Jonny*. The ratio is more than 4 to 30 for the backgrounds. Two animators are needed for every one on any other show."

At the time they launched *Jonny Quest*, Bill and Joe endeavored to produce a new *Wizard of Oz* series. *Dorothy and the Land of Oz* would have featured a real-life Dorothy and animated Tin Woodsman, Cowardly Lion, and Strawman. Bill and Joe launched a nationwide search for a 10-year-old girl to play Dorothy, but the show never came to pass. They had a dozen other projects in the works, including a series of specials. The first of these was the hour-long *Alice in Wonderland or What's a Nice Kid Like You Doing in a Place Like This?* Originally to debut that Thanksgiving or Christmas, the animated adaptation of Lewis Carroll's beloved children's tale premiered on March 30, 1966, on ABC. Scored by famed Broadway composers Lee Adams and Charles Strouse and voiced by Sammy Davis Jr., Zsa Zsa Gabor, Bill Dana, and others, this prime-time television event, in which Fred Flintstone and Barney Rubble also turn up as the front and rear ends of the Blue Caterpillar character, garnered an Emmy nomination for "Individual Achievement in Music."

Meanwhile, during the 1964–1965 season, Bill and Joe were dealt some disappointing news. ABC cancelled their beautifully drawn, carefully researched *Jonny Quest* series after only one season, at a huge financial loss of more than $500,000. Later, the series became a Saturday-morning favorite on CBS for three seasons.

That same season, *The Flintstones*, in its fifth season, also showed signs of age. It lost the ratings battle against a much tougher competitor scheduled opposite it on CBS: the live-action monster spoof *The Munsters*. "The funny thing is I tried to sell *The Gruesomes* to TV two years ago—with no takers," Joe said at the time.

Soon Bill and Joe would again be on the right side of history. Continuing their reign by creating more characters and top-rated shows for television than any other studio, they would carve out another niche earning them yet another distinction in their storied careers as "the sultans of Saturday morning."

7

Changing the Face of Saturday Morning Television

A lthough audiences loved their limited-animated shows, through the 1965–1966 season, the three major networks continued programming their Saturday-morning schedules with a mix of new and repackaged and recycled old theatrical cartoon favorites. This included two new half-hour programs Bill and Joe ushered onto the air—first airing independently of each other, then later as a one-hour block—called *The Atom Ant/Secret Squirrel Show*. It featured the invincible superhero ant and trench-coated squirrel (a parody of Ian Fleming's James Bond) in separate episodes. The following fall, the television landscape radically changed after Fred Silverman, a young, ambitious CBS daytime programming executive, revolutionized Saturday-morning by introducing the first all-cartoon schedule featuring fresh, new original shows loved by kids and advertisers alike.

Silverman introduced six new series, including Filmation's *The New Adventures of Superman*, Format Films's *The Lone Ranger*, and two that Bill and Joe produced, *Frankenstein Jr. and the Impossibles* and *Space Ghost and Dino Boy*, and catapulted CBS from third to first place. In fact,

Frankenstein Jr. and the Impossibles and *Space Ghost and Dino Boy* rewarded CBS with the best Saturday morning ratings it had ever posted, while *Space Ghost* garnered a phenomenal 55 percent audience share.

That season, fantasy and action/adventure shows became top draws as both ABC and NBC tried to compete. Bill and Joe revved up NBC's Saturday-morning programming that season with yet another fantasy/adventure series, *The Space Kidettes*. Hanna-Barbera dominated television that season with 18 half-hour shows airing weekly, including returning syndicated favorites and the newly animated *Laurel & Hardy*. With six other shows televised, including reruns of *The Magilla Gorilla Show* on CBS and *Top Cat* and *The Jetsons* on NBC, they competed with themselves on all three networks.

Now with 350 people on staff, Bill and Joe estimated they kept track of 78,000 separate scenes daily and had produced 352 stories since February 1966, 6,000 feet of animation a week, and as many as 20 cartoons each week. Explaining their success, Joe told *Los Angeles Times* columnist Charles Champlin, "We figure our audience starts at 4. By then the kids have the strength to turn on the set and change channels. And they're so smart then, so discriminating! You can't fool around with them or give them fairy tale stuff . . . You've got to be on top of the times. And not just for kids, either. I'm on a screaming campaign to make the point that cartoons are not just for kids. We've never done cartoons for kids, just for kids. They're for everybody."

In dreaming up new characters and premises, Joe noted that he and Bill relied on one simple prerequisite: "We ask ourselves, would you want to take this character to bed as a stuffed toy? If not, out it goes. Even our villains have to be friendly."

In a business as volatile as animation, Bill and Joe remained successful by respecting each other's abilities. As Joe stated, "First, we settle on a project. Once we do this, I talk to writers. Bill moves it in the plant. Bill takes the material, and if he thinks a voice isn't right, we change the voice. We start out agreeing on a project, and then separate our duties. We have so much to do, we don't have time for bickering."

That summer, Bill and Joe realized their plans of bringing *The Flintstones* to the big screen, something they had had in the works for some

The Flintstones, becoming the longest-running cartoon series of its time in prime-time, spawned the 1966 big-screen spy feature, *The Man Called Flintstone*. © Hanna-Barbera Productions.

time. Announcing the production that January, it became their studio's second full-length feature, a spy spoof titled *The Man Called Flintstone*. In this outing, their pen-and-ink prehistoric television favorites travel to Eurock where they encounter the agents of the dreaded underground spy organization SMISH. Released to theaters on August 3, 1966, the comedy caper did better in test runs than such live-action spy and action films as *The Silencers* and *Cat Ballou*, the latter a big moneymaker for Columbia Pictures. Unlike their first go-round, *Hey There, It's Yogi Bear*, made specifically for the family and kiddie market, this time they designed their Flintstones feature for adults. "We feel it's the first one done with this in mind," Bill explained then. "We've gone out for guts, laughs."

That September, *The Flintstones* ended its six-year reign as the longest-running prime-time cartoon series of its time. Translated into 17 languages and seen weekly in 47 foreign countries from Japan to Nova Scotia, the series was then rebroadcast on NBC from 1967 to 1970, spawning numerous Saturday-morning variations and spin-offs and television specials in the 1970s and 1980s. Between 1966 and 1967, Joe proposed an offshoot of *The Flintstones*, called *The Blackstones*, featuring an all-black Stone Age family as next-door neighbors to Fred and Wilma that, as he said, "no network or syndicator would touch" because it was "too provocative."

In December 1966, with their studio blossoming in size and profits, Bill and Joe sold their company to Taft Broadcasting Company of Cincinnati for $12 million, with Taft signing them both to long-term contracts—with Joe as president and Bill as senior vice-president—to continue managing the operation. Neither the sale nor changing times slowed down their enterprise in producing 25 cartoon shows, shown in 51 countries, and licensing more than 4,000 merchandise items tied in to their famous creations. The 1967 season marked the arrival of seven new shows, including *Abbott & Costello*, the half-hour animated antics of the famed film comedy duo (with aging straight-man Bud Abbott lending his voice) for first-run syndication, and six all action-adventure shows for Saturday mornings: *Fantastic Four* on ABC; *The Herculoids, Moby Dick and the Mighty Mightor,* and *Shazzan* on CBS; and *Birdman and the Galaxy Trio* and *Samson & Goliath* on NBC.

Then, on February 26, 1967, after first announcing the project in October 1964, Bill and Joe realized plans to produce television's first combined live-action and animated special with the premiere of *Jack and the Beanstalk* on NBC. Based on the popular children's fairy tale, it had been in the planning for over a year after they had announced the production and was originally to air around Thanksgiving or Christmas of 1966. The special starred Gene Kelly and blended real characters played by live actors with animated characters. Live performers portrayed Jack (Bobby Riha) and his friend, and a traveling peddler Jeremy Keen (Gene Kelly), who fast-talks the youngster into swapping his cow for a handful of "magical" beans. Cartoon characters, including the frightful Giant, appeared high up in the beanstalk in Cloudland. The hour-long colorcast special featured the voices of Ted Cassidy (the stone-faced butler, Lurch, from TV's *The Addams Family*) as the Giant, Marni Nixon (of *My Fair Lady* fame) as the singing voice of Princess Serena, and Janet Waldo as the character's speaking voice. It included seven original musical numbers by award-winning songwriters Sammy Cahn and Jimmy Van Heusen. The program did not disappoint, winning an Emmy for "Outstanding Children's Special."

Not everything with the Hanna-Barbera brand, however, translated into immediate success. The pair produced pilots for two live-action shows, neither of which sold: *We'll Take Manhattan*, a situation comedy about a young lawyer who helps a 140-year-old Indian chief and his tribe, costarring Dwayne Hickman (of *Dobie Gillis* fame) and rubbery-faced comedian Ben Blue (only the pilot aired on April 30, 1967), and *What's New, World*, an hour-long travel and adventure series.

PRODUCING TAMER SATURDAY-MORNING FARE

By the 1968–1969 season, an outpouring of public disdain over the violent content of Saturday-morning cartoons followed the shocking assassinations of civil rights leader Dr. Martin Luther King and Senator Robert Kennedy. In response, networks dropped the profitable fantasy/superhero genre in favor of nonviolent fare. Bill and Joe subsequently produced 11 half-hours of mostly milder and amusing adaptations of historical events or literary works. Making up nearly half of the networks' combined Saturday-morning schedules, the shows included: *The Adventures of Gulliver; The Wacky Races;* the studio's first-ever hosted live-action hour, *The Banana Splits Adventure Hour,* featuring a live band of bubblegum rockers and weekly live-action and animated segments; *Danger Island; Micro Ventures; Arabian Knights;* and *The Three Musketeers* (replaced by *The Hillbilly Bears,* previously shown on *The Atom Ant/Secret Squirrel Show,* in the second season).

Of these, *The Wacky Races* represented a major departure in terms of their approach and format. Inspired in part by two popular 1965 live-action comedies, *The Great Race* and *Those Magnificent Men in Their Flying Machines,* the half-hour comedy/adventure pitted 11 racing teams driving an unusual array of four-wheeled contraptions (designed by Iwao Takamoto) in a madcap cross-country racing competition. Central to the show was the nefarious, double-dealing Dick Dastardly and his snickering canine, Muttley, trying to win the old-fashioned way: by cheating. The program was such an enormous hit that it spawned two spin-offs in the 1969–1970 season: *Dastardly & Muttley in Their Flying Machines* (originally called *Stop the Pigeon*) and *The Perils of Penelope Pitstop*—based partly on an old movie serial, *The Perils of Pauline*—starring the beautiful blond Southern belle racing her Compact Pussycat car in international competitions.

The "most expensive" half-hour show Hanna-Barbera ever produced for prime-time that season was the combination live-action/animated series *The New Adventures of Huck Finn,* adapted from Mark Twain's famous characters for NBC. The 20-episode series, which aired Sunday evenings, followed the further adventures of Huck Finn, Becky Thatcher, and Tom Sawyer, thrusting them into various make-believe fantasy worlds with their surroundings animated and their characters in live-action. Costumes worn by Huck and Tom included high-gaiter shoes, in step with the late 1960s "mod" look.

Bill and Joe's unparalleled success of the previous 10 years played a big part in transforming television into a huge profit center, thanks to ballooning advertising revenue. In that time, Saturday morning advertising rates had mushroomed eight times over from $1,000 to

Named by CBS programming head Fred Silverman from the Frank Sinatra lyrics, "Dooby dooby do," Bill and Joe's trembling Great Dane and teenage mystery-solvers evolved into a Saturday-morning smash hit and one of the studio's most successful franchises after the debut of *Scooby-Doo, Where Are You!* (1969). © *Hanna-Barbera Productions.*

$9,200 per minute. By November 1969, gross annual revenue from advertisers for the three networks totaled $90 million, up from $40 million four to five years previously. Launching the 1969–1970 season, CBS served up five-and-half hours of cartoons, among them three new Hanna-Barbera shows: *Dastardly & Muttley in Their Flying Machines, The Perils of Penelope Pitstop,* and *Scooby-Doo, Where Are You!* ABC, meanwhile, offered four-and-a-half hours, including their hour-long *The Cattanooga Cats*, featuring episodes of *Motormouse & Autocat*, *Around the World in 79 Days*, and *It's the Wolf*, and NBC offered three hours, including reruns of *The Flintstones*, plus a second season of its live-action/animated *The Banana Splits Adventure Hour*. As John Culhane of *Newsweek* noted, "In other words, more than two-thirds of all the Saturday 'morning' time on the three major networks—13½ out of a combined total of 18 hours between 8 A.M. and 2 P.M.—is occupied by drawings that move (more or less)."

Once again, Hanna-Barbera had captured the lion's share of animated shows on the air. As Bill reflected, "When Joe and I made *Tom and Jerry*, we made about eight six-minute cartoons a year. That's about 48 minutes of animation a year. Now we're turning out 120 minutes a week. In other words, we're doing more than twice as much here every week as we used to do in a year at MGM."

Bill and Joe's ability to adapt to the ever-changing demands of the medium helped them not only endure but also flourish. "We can write adventure or go funny," Bill stated. "We've just finished 17 *Penelope Pitstops* . . . We write the *Penelopes* and the *Scoobys* in story form. Then a story director translates our idea into a storyboard. . . . "

COMING AT THE RIGHT TIME—A TREMBLING CANINE

The clear winner on CBS that season was *Scooby-Doo, Where Are You!* Premiering on September 13, 1969, right after *The Perils of Penelope Pitstop*, the comedy-mystery series starred the chicken-hearted Great Dane, Scooby-Doo, and a foursome of teenage detectives, Shaggy, Velma, Daphne, and Freddy, roaming the country in their psychedelic-colored Mystery Machine van. It scored a whopping 11.6 ratings, beating another Hanna-Barbera product, NBC's *The Banana Splits*, in its time slot. Fred Silverman, still CBS's head of daytime programming, had suggested the idea of a comedy-adventure combining two series he liked: Carlton E. Morse's popular radio detective program *I Love a Mystery*, and the CBS sitcom *The Many Loves of Dobie Gillis* (1959–1963), the adventures of "a scatterbrained teenager and his friends."

As Silverman later recalled of the show's development, "I had always thought that kids in a haunted house would be a big hit, played for laughs, in animation. And I developed a show with Hanna-Barbera. And there was a dog in there, but the dog was in the background; it was much more serious . . . And CBS President Frank Stanton says, 'We can't put that on the air, that's just too frightening.'" During a red-eye flight, the name for the character popped into Silverman's head while listening to Frank Sinatra ad-libbing the closing scat, "Dooby dooby doo," in his hit song "Strangers in the Night." As Silverman said, "It's at that point I said that's it, we'll take the dog— we'll call it Scooby-Doo." During preliminary discussions, studio layout artist/designer Iwao Takamoto suggested during a meeting with Joe that the canine be "a big, clumsy dog," thus settling on the breed of a Great Dane.

CBS made the show their centerpiece that fall. The teenage mystery was first titled *Mystery Five*, then *Who's Scared?* and finally *Scooby-Doo, Where Are You!* Writers Ken Spears and Joe Ruby created the characters designed by Iwao Takamoto. The show was an immediate smash hit. Earning exceptionally high ratings, *Scooby* aired for three seasons, becoming Hanna-Barbera's third most successful and longest-running franchise for 22 consecutive seasons on network television. That included two seasons of *The New Scooby-Doo Comedy Movies*, hour-long adventures featuring celebrity guests in cartoon form. In 1976, CBS did not pick up the show's option, and it moved to ABC, starting with the 90-minute *The Scooby-Doo/Dynomutt Hour*, where it became a permanent fixture on the network until the early 1990s. Variations included *The Scooby-Doo Show; Scooby's All-Star Laff-a-Lympics*, the first two-hour Saturday-morning show featuring Olympic-styled competitions; and *Scooby-Doo and Scrappy-Doo*, introducing Scooby's feisty little nephew.

Throughout the 1970s, Bill and Joe produced the bulwark of American-made television cartoon shows and occasional prime-time animated and Saturday-morning specials, with growing competition from Filmation, DePatie-Freleng Enterprises, and Ruby-Spears studios (founded by one-time Hanna-Barbera Production employees,

Cartoon legends Bill Hanna (left) and Joseph Barbera as they looked in animated form. © *Hanna-Barbera Productions.*

Ken Spears and Joe Ruby). After producing in 1970 a football comedy, *Where's Huddles?*, as a prime-time summer-time replacement show for CBS's *The Glen Campbell Goodtime Hour*, Hanna-Barbera enjoyed success with two new, family-oriented, mystery, action/adventure Saturday-morning shows in the mold of Scooby-Doo: *The Harlem Globetrotters*, and *Josie & the Pussycats*.

In 1971, ten years after the debut *The Flintstones*, their famous offspring, Pebbles and Bamm-Bamm, now teenagers, headlined their own show Saturday mornings on NBC, *Pebbles & Bamm-Bamm*. (As Joe, then 57, mused, "They're not really old enough to be teen-agers, but television makes people grow up faster.") Two more new shows joined the docket, *Help!...It's the Hair Bear Bunch!*—originally developed under the name *The Yo Yo Bears*—and *The Funky Phantom*.

In 1972, marking their 15th season of television and 35th year of their partnership, they tripled their sales to networks while only doubling their combined budgets to $12 million. On NBC that fall, Bill and Joe launched their latest Saturday-morning endeavor, *Sealab 2020*, a fact-based science series about an underwater city 50 years in the future, along with *The Roman Holidays*, a family sitcom in the style of *The Flintstones* but set in ancient Roman times, and *Amazing Chan & the Chan Clan*, an updated version of the *Charlie Chan* detective movie series on which it was based. Meanwhile, on CBS, the adolescent adventures of Pebbles and Bamm-Bamm was expanded into *The Flintstone Comedy Hour*.

Bill and Joe also returned to prime time, winning over viewers with a provocative family sitcom centered on the generation gap between an old-fashioned father, Harry Boyle (voiced by Tom Bosley) and his three modern-day children (Chet, Alice, and Jamie), *Wait Till Your Father Gets Home*. Beginning on September 12, the 48-episode first-run syndicated show, produced under the new FCC Prime-Time Access Rule restricting the amount of network programming that local network affiliates could broadcast during prime time, aired nationally on Friday nights at 7:30 in many major markets, including five owned and operated NBC affiliates. The series, created by Harvey Bullock and R. S. Allen, began as a one-shot animated half-hour, titled *Love and the Old-Fashioned Father*, on Paramount Television's popular nighttime adult sitcom on ABC, *Love American Style*. That episode also served as the pilot for the 1972–1974 syndicated cartoon series. Lasting two seasons, despite many critics labeling it "a thinly drawn copy of *All in the Family*," Joe insisted the father figure was not an Archie Bunker–type but rather "an old-fashioned father . . . who says the things all parents should be saying to their kids. Our father loves the mother. And the mother is not a kook. And the father is not a screaming stoop."

GROWING THEIR CARTOON EMPIRE

That same season, Bill and Joe also ventured into new territory, producing their first live-action film, a quirky period Western about a soldier of fortune (Clint Walker) whose wife has run off with a Mexican revolutionary, *Hardcase*, for ABC. That October, the first *ABC Afterschool Special* aired, *The Last of the Curlews*, produced by Hanna-Barbera. A beautifully animated ecology story of the last existing members of this bird species, the special won an Emmy in 1973 for "Outstanding Achievement in Children's Programming."

Following its success, Bill and Joe produced many seasonal specials that garnered high viewership. The first of these in 1971 were *The Thanksgiving That Almost Wasn't* and *A Christmas Story*, followed in 1972 by *Robin Hoodnik* and *Oliver Twist and the Artful Dodger*. Hanna-Barbera also produced ABC's third animation presentation for its *Afterschool Special* series, *Cyrano* (1974), an adaptation of the life of Cyrano de Bergerac (voiced by José Ferrer) and nominated that year for an Emmy. They also turned out cartoon versions of highly rated live-action series: *Gidget Makes the Wrong Connection* (1972), *Lost in Space* (1972), and a second episode of ABC's nighttime adult sitcom *Love American Style*, coproduced by Alan Rafkin, called *Love and the Private Eye* (1972). Hanna-Barbera likewise dabbled in doing a series of specials based on classic children's stories and literary figures up through 1979, including *The Count of Monte Cristo*, *20,000 Leagues Under the Sea*, *Last of the Mohicans*, *Davy Crockett on the Mississippi*, *Five Weeks in a Balloon*, *Black Beauty*, and *Gulliver's Travels*.

Expanding their efforts to produce full-length animated features, Bill and Joe were also busy putting the finishing touches on their third feature adapted from E. B. White's beloved 1952 children's book, *Charlotte's Web*. The film was originally scheduled for worldwide release at Christmas in 1972 and in the United States the following Easter. Bill and Joe coproduced the estimated $1.5 million adaptation with Edgar Bronfman's Sagittarius Productions; Bronfman was responsible for persuading White, who had held out for 15 years, to sell the film rights to the property. Earl Hamner Jr. was assigned to write the film script, "changing it as little as possible."

Starting with *Charlotte's Web*, their plan was to produce another feature, either animated or live-action, before the end of 1972, and produce one animated feature and two live-action pictures in 1973.

If successful, they intended to increase their output to a total of five features a year. This was in addition to 24 new projects for Saturday-morning television and 18 live-action projects for prime-time television which were then in development. Methods of selling their shows had changed from Joe pitching them from storyboards and acting out all the characters for prospective sponsors and giving as many as five presentations a day to networks. "I used to practically live in an airplane between here and New York," Joe recalled. "Going east I'd draw one complete storyboard for a show, and coming west I'd draw another. We both worked continually. At least now I can sandwich in part of a movie between work. I no longer draw much, but I have plenty of reading to do."

Part of Hanna-Barbera's assembly line now included the process of Xerography. "Previously every drawing had to be done by hand," Joe said, "but now we can photograph them onto a cell . . . With all the red lights and machines, the place looks like Dante's Inferno." Hanna-Barbera employed 600 staffers working 20 hours a day through two long shifts at the company's cramped Cahuenga Boulevard studio and another smaller facility in nearby Burbank, with other staffers in Bill's and Joe's home offices. This was until a planned $1 million addition, almost doubling the studio's size to 75,000 square feet, was completed. Expansion also included featuring the studio's widely known characters and others of their creation at Taft Broadcasting's King's Park amusement parks in Cincinnati and under construction in Virginia (with a television set façade called "The Happy Kingdom of Hanna-Barbera"). As Joe stated, in publicizing production of *Charlotte's Web* in September 1972, "We took a much shorter time to do it than Disney would. An animated feature takes up to four years at Disney. We did ours in 16 months." E. B. White retained the right of approval for the spider drawings based on his exquisite artwork and beautiful spider. Bill and Joe flew to White's home in Maine where he drew a sketch of Charlotte and, in Joe's word, "we took it from there."

Despite all the advanced promotional buildup, Bill and Joe's theatrical version "suffered from the taint of limited animation and questionable production values." The film opened in movie theaters on

Bill and Joe's plans to expand their production of full-length features, live-action or animated, started with this adaptation of E. B. White's classic children's novel, *Charlotte's Web* (1973). © *Hanna-Barbera Productions.*

March 1, 1973. Critics dismissed it for many of the same reasons. *New York Times* critic Vincent Canby opined, "Parents will survive it, and so will the children." Joe later acknowledged that he and Bill may have misjudged the "financial potential of the material." As he explained, "'Charlotte's Web' is an American classic. It is not an all-world classic. Germany ended up calling it 'Zuckerman's Pig,' after the name of the man who owned the pig in the story, because who ever heard of a 'Charlotte's Web?'" Despite the box-office disappointment, the studio managed to recoup some of its production costs in the future through the sale of television rights to HBO, home video cassettes, and its release in nontheatrical markets.

Bill and Joe returned to producing an even larger slate of original programs for Saturday morning over the next two seasons. In 1973, they produced spin-offs of hit prime-time sitcoms, one-season wonders, and the return of the comic-book superhero genre in the form of *Jeannie; Speed Buggy; The Addams Family; Goober and the Ghost Chasers; Inch High, Private Eye; Butch Cassidy & the Sundance Kids;* and *Super Friends,* a realistic action/adventure series starring famed comic-book superheroes Superman, Batman and Robin, Wonder Woman, Aquaman, and others. Beginning a 12-year reign on Saturday morning, the series proved a durable top-rated franchise for the studio in different variations. The following season, they sought to appeal to both young and teenage audiences with *Hong Kong Phooey, These Are the Days, Devlin, Valley of the Dinosaurs, Wheelie and the Chopper Bunch,* and *Partridge Family: 2200 A.D.*

In 1973, after NBC acquired the broadcast rights to NHL hockey games, Hanna-Barbera Productions gave life to an animated mascot, named Peter Puck. The "know-it-all spokesman for the game" presented hockey in a more interesting fashion during intermissions of the network's *Hockey Game of the Week*. The NHL games were languishing third in the ratings behind ABC's family sports and CBS's NBA basketball games, and Scott Connal, executive producer of NBC Sports, decided a mascot would create more interest among viewers, who he said "wouldn't sit still for many more blackboard presentations." So he called Joe Barbera, who created the oval-shaped puck character off the top of his head, with actor Ronnie Schell lending his voice to acquaint viewers with rules and basics of "the fastest game on ice."

Peter Puck was introduced during the first intermission period of an Atlanta Flames hockey game. He slid down a cartoon ice surface and piped up, "Hey, cool it fellas," after an orange hockey stick made an impromptu slapshot while he was talking. Peter became an immediate hit. For two years he was featured in three-minute segments on NBC's *NHL Game of the Week* and for five more on CBC's *Hockey Night in Canada*, with response to his character producing an extraordinary stampede of Peter Puck tee-shirts, watches, and dolls. The peculiar-looking character did not escape the wrath of some critics, though. With hockey a predominantly Canadian sport, one writer complained, "Couldn't you please change his name from Peter to Pierre?"

A year later, Bill and Joe added more live-action productions to the fold. In the 1973–1974 season, they offered, *The Runaways*, an ABC *Afterschool Special* that won an Emmy for "Outstanding Information Children's Special." Proving themselves as contenders in the live-action film business, they combined their classic storytelling ability, demonstrated for nearly two decades in making cartoons, producing additional live-action specials for network television during the next three seasons, including *Shoot-Out in a One Dog Town* for ABC, and *The Phantom Rebel* for NBC, as well as straight live-action shows for Saturday morning, among them, ABC's *Korg: 70,000 B.C.* and NBC's *Mystery Island*.

SOMETHING OLD, SOMETHING BORROWED, AND SOMETHING NEW

With five shows returning or airing in reruns in 1975, that September, 35 years after their creation, Bill and Joe revived their famous cat-and-mouse characters in a new series of cartoons, *The Tom & Jerry Show*, for ABC in association with Metro-Goldwyn-Mayer Television. Combined with episodes of a new arrival, a gigantic purple *Grape Ape* (subsequently retitled, *The New Tom & Jerry/Grape Ape Show*), the pair appeared in 48 toned-down, nonviolent, seven-minute adventures renewing their rivalry as "the best of friends" in assorted misadventures. Audiences longed for the old theatrical shorts, and the show lasted only one season.

Bill (left) and Joe display their Annie Award won in the producer's category in 1977. *(Courtesy: Raymond Cox.)* © Raymond Cox. All rights reserved.

By the following year, while exerting their creative energies producing new Saturday-morning fare—*Dynomutt, Dog Wonder; Jabberjaw; Mumbly;* and *Clue Club*—Bill and Joe were honored with their very own star on the Hollywood Walk of Fame. A year later, Hollywood's International Animated Film Society (ASIFA) awarded them the Winsor McCay lifetime achievement award. Bill and Joe were back in high gear that season, turning out 10,000 feet of processed film a week and eight new Saturday-morning shows, including *The C.B. Bears; Shake, Rattle & Roll; Undercover Elephant; Heyyy, It's The King; Wonder Wheels; Blast Off Buzzard; Captain Caveman and the Teen Angels;* and *Posse Impossible.* At that same time they were in the second year of a program they had launched in October 1976 to train young animators, a so-called college of animation.

With the production season lasting only six months, like other studios, Bill and Joe had a hard time recruiting animators to fill jobs that were not year-round. They started the program, as Joe said, to "train people if the industry is going to continue." By September 1977, 103 men and women had completed the program. Joe had convinced Taft Broadcasting Company to fund four animated feature films to be made over a five-year period to provide steady work for their employees; as a result, many of their trainees were soon working at the studio. Held four nights a week at the studio, the college was run by veteran animator Harry Love, who screened applicants. Those showing promise were invited to attend classes while some applicants were given apprentice jobs right away. By that year, the total number of employees at Hanna-Barbera had reached 2,000.

In 1978, still carrying a heavy workload for men pushing their late sixties, Bill and Joe muscled through 30 grueling weeks producing a host of new Saturday-morning offerings: *The Robonic Stooges, The Galaxy Goof-Ups, The Galloping Ghost, The Buford Files, Godzilla, Jana of the Jungle, The All-New Popeye Hour,* and *Dinky Dog.* That season, Yogi Bear, still drawing big audiences, made history with two different series on the network schedules at the same time: *Yogi's Space Race* and *Galaxy Goof-Ups.* That same year their fifth live-action movie for ABC television, *The Gathering* (1977), starring Ed Asner and Maureen Stapleton, won an Emmy. This was one of several live-action films developed for television: *It Isn't Easy Being a Teenage Millionaire* (1978), *The Beasts Are on the Streets* (1978), *KISS Meets the Phantom of the Park* (1978), and sequel, *The Gathering: Part II* (1979). Bill and Joe also released *C.H.O.M.P.S.* (1979), their first live-action theatrical feature. The comedy/adventure was about a boy who invents a robotic dog that thwarts burglars, cowritten by Joe and released by American International Pictures.

Even for the usually calm and reserved Bill Hanna, the pace became too much to handle. "Every morning I was in the office by 8 A.M. and I never got home before 8 at night," Bill recalled. "Usually I'd call my wife to meet me somewhere for dinner. Saturdays I put in about eight hours and Sundays I went a little easier, only about six hours. I swore at the end of the season I'd never do it again."

Years of criticism from television critics, parental groups, and their peers about the quality and craftsmanship of their productions never ceased. Oscar-winning animator Chuck Jones dismissed Hanna-Barbera and other producers of limited animation as "illustrated radio." During a later interview with Eugene Slafer, when asked, "Are you accomplishing what you believe is good TV animation?" Bill said, "No, I do not."

After delving further and asking if he was ever ashamed of his work and the overall lack of quality of Saturday-morning cartoon programs, he confessed, "Actually I feel like I should crawl under a seat sometimes."

Though Bill was quick in his assessment to recognize the difference between good and poor quality animation, during an interview in 1981, Joe was much more defensive. "We had to get that stuff out for Saturday morning," he noted. "That's a budget problem. Believe me, I don't stand still for people saying, 'Oh, they're doing junk! They don't know how to do . . .' We're not doing that. We only do it because you don't get the money to do it differently. When we get the money—and you're talking about millions—we do a job!"

Despite working long and hard, Bill enjoyed whatever downtime he had in the great outdoors—fishing off a 53-foot motor boat, on camping trips, and at his two-story ranch house on a 150-acre spread in the Fall River Valley region of Northern California. Joe, who disliked fishing and camping, preferred basking in the warm weather and sunshine of his villa, which was among many million-dollar estates on West Camino Norte in Palm Springs. The household included a private swimming pool, tennis court, and a large orchard of grapefruit and lemon trees, with majestic views of the San Jacinto Mountains.

Neither enjoyed much of a respite the following season as Fred Silverman, who left ABC in 1978 to become president and CEO of NBC, ordered five new series and renewed one with plans to rebroadcast two more, *The Adventures of Jonny Quest* and *The Jetsons*, for a total of eight shows that fall. ABC renewed two other Hanna-Barbera shows, *The Plastic Man Comedy/Adventure Show* and *Scooby-Doo and Scrappy-Doo*, and

Joe holds up a production cel from NBC's new 30-minute Saturday-morning series, *The New Fred and Barney Show* (1979). © *Hanna-Barbera Productions.*

CBS renewed one, *The All-New Popeye Hour*, with 11 shows altogether on the air. One major complaint Joe had of the process was, unlike the days when they had complete control between the idea and development of a property, they had to account to 15 people. As he said, "That I'm not happy about."

That February, *The Flintstones* returned to the small screen on NBC in a 30-minute Saturday-morning series revival Bill and Joe produced, called *The New Fred and Barney Show*. The new show featured a new family, The Frightenstones, an animated *Addams Family* knock-off. The show also marked the debut of actor Henry Corden as the voice of Fred Flintstone, replacing the character's original voice man, Alan Reed, who died in June 1977. Then, in the fall, featured on NBC's Saturday-morning docket were *Casper and the Angels*, *Fred and Barney Meet the Thing*, *The Super Globetrotters*, *The New Shmoo*, and *Godzilla*. Meanwhile, ABC's premiere of *Scooby-Doo and Scrappy-Doo* marked Scooby-Doo's 11th year on television, with Hanna-Barbera's contract with the network guaranteeing its stay on the air until 1985.

In remarkable careers already highlighted by many important milestones, just when it appeared they had no new heights to climb, Bill and Joe once again found themselves on the right side of history.

New Beginnings

With NBC deep in third place and considering dropping its Saturday-morning children's programming altogether, Bill and Joe made television history again. One day in 1979, network president Fred Silverman called offering them an on-the-air commitment if they could secure the rights to a brand of little blue people that had caught the attention of his young daughter. They were also enjoying widespread popularity and through-the-roof merchandise sales in America. As Silverman said, "Get the rights to the Smurfs."

Bill and Joe did exactly that, obtaining the rights to French cartoonist Peyo Culliford's popular Belgian comic strip. Two years later, they introduced to Saturday-morning audiences *The Smurfs*, a 60-minute series that followed the magical tales of the wise Papa Smurf and his happy, hyperactive crew of busybodies who make their homes in mushrooms. The Smurfs featured Brainy, Vanity, Hefty, Clumsy, Jokey, Greedy, Lazy, Handy, Grouchy, Harmony, and Smurfette. Rocketing NBC to the top of the ratings heap, *The Smurfs* became the highest-rated Saturday-morning show in eight years and the highest for an NBC animated program since 1970. A favorite of children and parents alike, *The Smurfs* broke new ground by offering positive messages about serious subjects—drug abuse, physical handicaps, prejudice, and death—without being preachy.

At the urging of then NBC programming chief Fred Silverman, Bill and Joe secured the rights to produce what would become one of Saturday-morning's highest-rated and longest-running series, based on cartoonist Peyo Culliford's famed Belgian comic-strip, *The Smurfs* (1981). © *Hanna-Barbera Productions.*

The show expanded to an unprecedented 90 minutes in 1982. During its 10-season run, Bill and Joe were awarded their sixth and seventh Emmys for "Outstanding Animated Program (Daytime)" in 1982 and 1983, and were nominated for a trio of prime-time half-hour specials, *The Smurf Springtime Special* (1982), *The Smurfs Christmas Special* (1982), and *The Smurfic Games* (1984). During these years Bill and Joe also produced a mix of old and new characters and spin-offs of popular live-action prime-time comedies for Saturday morning, including *The Fonz and the Happy Days Gang, Richie Rich, The Tom and Jerry Comedy Show, Kwicky Koala, Laverne & Shirley in the Army, The Popeye and Olive Show, The Trollkins, Pac-Man,* and many others.

By 1981, Bill and Joe pushed forward with earlier plans to produce high-quality, family-friendly, full-length animated features. As Joe stated, "The thrust was to do one [feature] every year and to build a superb perennial library, which Disney had done for years," Joe stated. Unlike their limited-animated series and previous low-cost features, these would be exquisitely animated like Disney's were, starting with a property in production since 1976 that Joe coscripted. It was their studio's fourth feature, *Heidi's Song.*

Their most expensive product to date, the film took five long years, at a cost of $9 million, to complete. The production boasted more than 200 artisans, including several old-timers who had "cut their teeth" working at MGM alongside Bill and Joe, such as Irv Spence, Ed Barge, and Preston Blair. Other animators who worked on the film included Hal Ambro and Charlie Downs, specialists in human figure animation on Disney's *Peter Pan* and Richard Williams's *Raggedy Ann & Andy.* Bill and Joe assumed they could keep their crew busy working on the feature during the slow season or downtime of production of their ongoing television commitments. But as Joe admitted, "We found that doesn't work. The first three or four years the picture would go into production and stop, then go back into production and then stop. That was not good for the picture. We were losing momentum, the enthusiasm of the artists and the excitement we wanted to build up."

They changed directors midstream, replacing skilled Hanna-Barbera cartoon auteur Charles A. Nichols with Robert Taylor. Taking over the already scripted project with vocal tracks also recorded proved far more difficult. As Taylor related, "It was a hang-up for me . . . I would have made it a little stronger in terms of her [Heidi's] emotions and some of the dialogue."

Bill and Joe stretched their studio thin trying to produce its exploding slate of television cartoons besides *Heidi's Song* and two other features: *Rock Odyssey*, a "rock-'Fantasia'" as Joe called it, and *Nessie Come Home*, the story of the famed Loch Ness monster. They also announced plans for another feature, *Pirate Jack*, "going beyond 'Yellow Submarine,'" that never materialized. The productions were meant to maximize box-office sales by basing them on characters "people will identify with."

Originally to be released in the summer of 1981, *Heidi's Song* finally premiered, on November 19, 1982, at Hollywood's Grauman's Chinese Theatre the same weekend as *Bugs Bunny's Third Movie: 1001 Rabbit Tales* and *The Last Unicorn*. It received generally high marks: *Los Angeles Times* critic Linda Gross called the film "well crafted" and acceptable for "the youngest toddlers," and *New York Times* critic Janet Maslin wrote "a better film for small children than older ones." Yet not even an all-star voice cast (Lorne Greene and Sammy Davis Jr.), beautifully crafted animation, and 15 original songs by songwriters Sammy Cahn and Burton Lane could save the 94-minute, full-color feature from disaster. Producing what they hoped would become their first "classic" feature à la Disney's *Snow White and the Seven Dwarfs*, the movie grossed a meager $5.1 million in its release.

The failure of *Heidi's Song* forced Bill and Joe to shut down their feature animation unit. *Nessie Come Home* was never completed, while *Rock Odyssey* was. Financed and commissioned by ABC as a prime-time television special, the weird musical was shelved by Taft Broadcasting executives. After reviewing the first five reels, they deemed its graphic imagery, particularly covering the 1960s and Vietnam War, "too realistic." After Taylor departed, Bill and Joe instructed title sequence director Bill Perez to jettison the objectionable footage and add a new sequence featuring classic Hanna-Barbera cartoon clips set to the song "Wake Me

A scene from what Bill and Joe hoped would be remembered as their studio's first "classic" cartoon feature like Disney's *Snow White and the Seven Dwarfs*, the book-to-screen adaptation that instead was a box-office disaster, *Heidi's Song* (1982). © *Hanna-Barbera Productions*.

Up Before You Go-Go" by the band Wham!, and other songs up to the 1980s to bring the project up-to-date.

A studio trade ad in the fall of 1981 promoted that ABC would air the special in the spring of 1982, but it never did. Bill and Joe sank $2 million into the production. The final film is a hodgepodge, through-the-decades history of rock 'n' roll with a soundtrack covering four decades of classic rock. Scatman Crothers, as the voice of a living juke-box, narrates—bridged together by the story of a young woman (Laura) who embarks on a journey to find love. It was shown only once in July 1987 at the Second World Animation Celebration at the Nuart Theater. *Los Angeles Times* critic Charles Solomon panned the musical epic as "animation's equivalent of 'Howard the Duck'" and "staggeringly terrible."

RETURNING TO THEIR ROOTS, TESTING NEW FRONTIERS

Bill and Joe's latest endeavor in prime-time television did not fare well either. Beginning on April 23, 1982, NBC aired their new series in the 8:00 P.M. hour not "just for kiddies" but also for the whole family: *Joke-book*. Based on the premise "life is a jokebook," the half-hour anthology, featuring material from various sources, consisted of a series of cute and absurd cartoon blackouts and skits. Praising its premiere episode, *New York Times* critic John J. O'Connor found it "more suited to a film course perhaps than the competitive mire of prime-time television," as did many other critics as well as viewers.

Between 1983 and 1984, with networks facing growing competition from cable networks and independent television stations airing cartoon programs based on popular toys, video games, and greeting card characters, Bill and Joe dished out many other Saturday-morning network and syndicated shows, some more popular than others, including *The Dukes, Monchhichis, The Biskitts, The Snorks, The Pink Panther and Sons,* and *Challenge of the GoBots.* Then, in 1985, they carved out a whole new marketplace—syndicated programming for Sunday morning—with an innovative block of original half-hour shows, *The Funtastic World of Hanna-Barbera*. Originally comprised of three newly animated half-hours—*Yogi's Treasure Hunt, The Paw Paws*, and *Galtar and the Golden Lance*—this 90-minute compendium was expanded to two hours in its second season and showed rotating cartoon fare in subsequent seasons through the 1992–1993 season. Other cartoons included *The Flintstone Kids*, originally produced for ABC in 1986, *Sky Commanders, The Snorks, The Further Adventures of Super Ted, Fantastic Max, Richie Rich*, and new weekly adventures of *Jonny Quest*.

Despite growing pressures to produce high-quality programming for television networks and syndication, Joe felt animation was "better than it ever was as TV cartoons used to consist of one character walking in front of a simple background. Now the networks want characters all over the screen. That's suicide to us, but we do it."

Joe admitted neither he nor Bill relied on polls, market tests, or research like networks did to gauge children's reactions and determine whether their ideas would be loved by the mainstream. "I go strictly by my own gut reaction," he said. "I go back to all those fabulous comedians. They never ran a test on anything. They did what they felt was right."

That same year, Bill and Joe entered the computer age, spending $10 million on cutting-edge technology—video camera, computer scanning, and coloring equipment—to facilitate creating cartoons, speed up production, and cut costs. In September, their studio employed the new computer-aided animation techniques, resulting in a smoother look and crisper sound, on six of 41 all-new episodes of *The Jetsons*. The new episodes joined the original 1962 series episodes in a first-run syndicated package that began airing on television stations across the country and spawned a remarkable resurgence. "Their popularity really amazes me," Joe remarked at the time. "It keeps getting stronger and stronger. Their theme song is being sung all over the country."

In the spring of 1986, Joe, at age 75, produced a new direct-to-home video series, culminating a 17-year dream to create animated Bible stories. The series was an outgrowth of his interest in great biblical stories from his days as a third grader at Holy Innocents School in Brooklyn. That April, at a cost of $2 million, Hanna-Barbera issued the first six half-hour videocassettes of *The Greatest Adventure: Stories from the Bible*, with another 20 videocassettes in development. Distributed by Worldvision Home Video, the video series, sold through religious bookstores and mail-order television advertising, racked up advance sales of 250,000 to 300,000 copies of the first six videos, becoming the most successful original children's video series of its time. Produced in cooperation with an advisory board of theologians of all faiths, each volume focused on the basic theme of "a belief in God."

Back in 1969, Joe first proposed a Bible project to the major networks and television syndicators with a drawing of David and Goliath as part of his pitch, but they declined. "You say Bible," Joe said, "and the networks get nervous." At that time networks were under siege by the FCC and parents groups for the airing of super-violent cartoons with "superheroes tangling with super-insidious villains" and facing pressure to air more educational shows on Saturday morning. But educational shows lost millions. Joe was happy the project had not sold then, fearful the studio would have lost money as well. "And I couldn't do it according to the Bible and stay within TV's rules," he said.

As a religious revival swept the country in the mid-1980s, Joe decided to go the home video and direct-sales route instead. The series was honored with the Golden Eagle Award (1988), National Religious Broadcasters Distinguished Service Award, Religion in Media's Gold Angel Award, and Film Advisory Board's Award of Excellence. In promoting the series at a convention of Catholic educators in Anaheim, California, Joe, baptized and raised Catholic, told the throng, "I was looking for the nun who used to whack me when I was 8 at Holy Innocents in Brooklyn. One nun told me I probably deserved it."

In the fall of 1986, Saturday morning, the bastion of network cartoons for some 20 years, came under serious attack as a plethora of first-run weekly and weekend syndicated series saturated the airwaves vying for advertising dollars. Bill and Joe were front and center in the midst of this storm. Their studio, along with Ruby-Spears (both owned by Taft Entertainment), accounted for more than 300 half-hours of cartoon programs—50 percent for Saturday morning, 50 percent for first-run

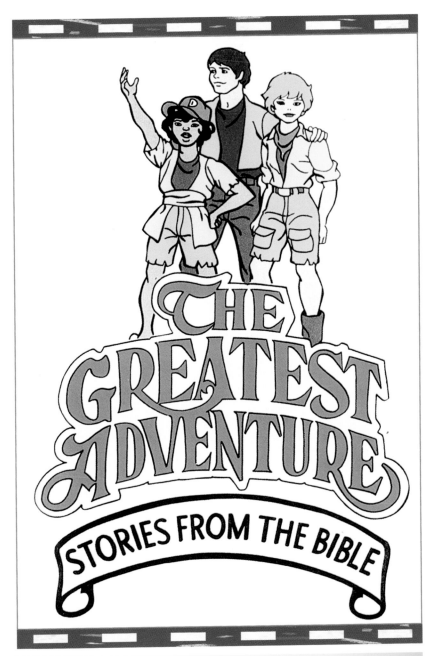

Artwork for Hanna-Barbera's best-selling direct-to-video *The Greatest Adventure: Stories from the Bible* series produced in 1986. © *Hanna-Barbera Productions.*

Bill (right) and Joe are honored at the August 1988 Emmy Awards by the Academy of Television Arts & Sciences with its lifetime achievement award, the Governors Award. © *Academy of Television Arts & Sciences.*

syndication—representing five different shows and two mini-series and a new roundup of Hanna-Barbera shows for Saturday morning. Out of all of them, the toy-inspired *Challenge of the GoBots* became the 18th-ranked, most-watched syndicated children's show. The series spawned a full-length feature that Bill and Joe also executive produced in March of that year, *GoBots: War of the Rock Lords.*

In 1987, as kids turned their backs on toy-driven cartoon characters and metal-faced cartoon warriors, Bill and Joe stormed back into the lucrative prime-time television arena by producing *Hanna-Barbera's Superstars 10*. The package of 10 two-hour movie specials was made over two seasons. It starred, in new adventures, the studio's most famous characters: The Flintstones, The Jetsons, Huckleberry Hound, Scooby-Doo, Top Cat, and others. Syndicated by Worldvision and sold as of August 1987 to more than 70 percent of the country's television markets, the production became their studio's most significant nighttime television exposure since *The Flintstones*. Part of the appeal of the series, Joe pointed out, was "Our shows have no death raids, no creatures from outer space, no characters with half-metal faces that talk in low, growly voices. Our characters are warm. We just have fun, and people are searching for that again."

CELEBRATING 50 YEARS OF PARTNERSHIP

Reaching the half-century mark of their partnership, on August 18, 1988, the award-winning pair was honored at the 40th annual Emmy Awards with the prestigious Governors Award for career achievement in television. Three decades since the debut of their first television series, *The Ruff and Reddy Show*, Bill and Joe had produced and/or directed almost 300 series totaling more than 1,500 hours of programming—an amount equal to 1,000 feature films—airing in some 80 countries and winning seven Emmys, a Humanitas Award, a Golden Globe, and star on the Hollywood Walk of Fame. Explaining the success of their long partnership, Joe stated, "We lean toward different areas of the business, so we each get to do what we like. I work on creating the ideas for projects and trying to sell those ideas to various markets. Bill oversees the actual production in studios all over the world, which I would hate doing." Of course, as he joked, "When Bill's out of town, I turn the light out behind his name on the studio sign, but he does the same thing to me when I'm gone, so we stay even."

For the silvery-haired Bill, the early years of running Hanna-Barbera studios were "more fun." As he confessed, "I was working more in creative areas of timing and direction then. But as the studio grew, I became more involved in administration and got away from

Bill (right) and Joe celebrate 50 years of partnership with their world-famous creations. © *Hanna-Barbera Productions*.

the creative aspects." With networks becoming more involved in the "creative process" requiring more input from the studio, he added, "Frankly, I miss that."

Three days after receiving with their special Emmy, Bill and Joe, both now 77, were celebrated with a special reception at the Circle Gallery in the Old Town district of San Diego launching of a series of autographed animation cels, priced from $600 to $700. The cels featured their famous cartoon creations: Yogi Bear and Boo Boo, Huckleberry Hound, The Flintstones, and The Jetsons. Joe, who thought of them all as his "children," was delighted by the outpouring of fans that came. "Everywhere we go, people line up out the door and tell us, 'We love Yogi Bear' They want to know, 'Where's Augie Doggie?' Our children are such lovable characters."

In 1989, Bill and Joe were busier than ever producing more original programs, including two prime-time specials, the first airing on September 15 on ABC, *The Flintstone Kids' "Just Say No,"* and a second on November 1 on CBS, an adaptation of Dik Browne's popular comic-strip Viking, *Hagar the Horrible*. They were also readying 44 new episodes of *The New Yogi Bear Show*, a half-hour weekday series starring Yogi and Boo Boo, a fourth season of *The Snorks* for first-run syndication beginning in 1987, and two new Saturday-morning series debuting that fall: *The Completely Mental Misadventures of Ed Grimley* (NBC) and *A Pup Named Scooby-Doo* (ABC).

That fall, after famed Hollywood producer David Kirschner was appointed president and chief executive to steer Bill and Joe's company, they agreed to create a prime-time television version of Stephen Spielberg's animated film *An American Tail*. They also agreed to produce with Spielberg's Amblin Entertainment a full-length live-action movie of *The Flintstones* commencing in April 1990. That May, a new attraction opened at Universal Studios's Florida theme park featuring Bill and Joe's world-famous characters in costume called "The Futuristic World of Hanna-Barbera." Meanwhile, on July 6, they were thrust back into the national spotlight following the release of their first feature in 24 years that they had produced and directed. *The Jetsons: The Movie* used computer-generated imagery (CGI) animation and reminded fans of the family of cartoon favorites Bill and Joe had created.

Bill (left) and Joe are all smiles at a fall 1989 book signing of the illustrated history, *The Art of Hanna-Barbera*. *(Courtesy: Raymond Cox.)*

The new feature revolved around a family-oriented storyline
entwined with an environmental message but with a contemporary
look. George was holding a new job as vice president of Spacely Sprockets and was adjusting with his family to their new home at Spacely's
Orbiting-Ore Asteroid. The film marked the final voice performances
of George O'Hanlon (George Jetson) and Mel Blanc (Mr. Spacely), and
the debuts of pop star Tiffany as the new voice of Judy, and Don Messick as Astro (replacing Daws Butler, who died in 1988). The film, met
by mixed reviews, was a financial disappointment. Opening fourth that
weekend to *Die Hard 2: Die Harder*, *Days of Thunder*, and *Dick Tracy*,

Advertisement for Bill and Joe's full-length animated feature based on their original 1962 futuristic prime-time sitcom, *Jestons: The Movie* (1990). © *Hanna-Barbera Productions.*

the cartoon feature grossed better than $5 million, but lost 43 percent of its audience the following weekend and took in only $20.3 million during its domestic theatrical run.

Despite their advancing age, neither Bill nor Joe slowed down. As Joe once said, a typical workday for them never really ended but was a "continuation of the day before. I keep carrying forward all the projects." At any given time, they had 6 to 26 different projects in various stages of development. One such project he pointed to during an interview were storyboard drawings of Tom and Jerry as kids. "They're cuter and rounder," Joe said. This version of the characters was for a new show for FOX, *Tom and Jerry Kids*. Debuting on March 2, 1990, the half-hour series lasted three seasons featuring two new adventures starring the famous cartoon duo and one featuring either former MGM mainstays Droopy and his new sidekick, Dripple, or Spike and Tyke.

Toned down from the classic *Tom and Jerry* cartoons, the characters in the new ones did not resort to simple chasing, but the new series raised the same criticism about it being too violent, something that baffled both creators, especially Joe. "I don't like it when organizations spring up and tell you what children should look at. Turn on the television anytime and there's a steady roll of car crashes, disasters, wife beatings. But cartoons? Slapstick and gags? I want to make kids laughs, adults laugh, and that's better than any medicine."

Preceding their latest cat-and-mouse incarnation, Bill and Joe agreed to produce the first full-length *Tom and Jerry* feature. It was a coproduction of Turner Entertainment Company, Media Special International, and Film Roman (producers of TV's *Garfield and Friends* and *Bobby's World*), with founder Phil Roman serving as the film's producer and director. In September 1987, they had first announced their plans, in partnership with DIC Entertainment, in which both characters would "talk," but that deal fell through. A year later, Joe met with media mogul Ted Turner, after he bought the rights to the entire MGM film library, including *Tom and Jerry*, in Atlanta, to pitch his idea of a theatrical *Tom and Jerry* film. Turner bought the idea in 15 minutes.

Subsequently, a new deal was struck between Turner Entertainment Co. and Film Roman.

Titled *Tom and Jerry: The Movie*, the 83-minute film started production in October 1990, with its original release date set for the summer of 1992. Joe was his normally effusive self, stating, "Tom and Jerry have always had a lot to say. Luckily, they've finally found the right script to put their thoughts into words for them." Unlike the MGM cartoon series, a cast of human characters, along with a variety of new and unusual supporting cartoon characters, would also populate their world.

Wrapping production, *Tom and Jerry: The Movie* opened in first-run theaters in Europe that October. During a publicity junket overseas, while attending a screening in Berlin, Joe received a prolonged standing ovation from a packed house of filmgoers. "It staggered me," he admitted. "It was embarrassing." For the film's opening in Paris that week, Joe conducted 22 interviews that Thursday and Friday alone. As a result of its success in Europe, a sequel was planned before the movie opened in the United States in July 1993, the 50th anniversary of their characters' creation. A series of 65 new half-hour episodes was set to air on television as well. Plans were also underway for another feature, *Droopy, The Master Detective*, which instead became a new, 13-episode, half-hour Saturday-morning series for FOX. Despite all this, the Tom and Jerry sequel was never produced.

TURNING OVER THE REIGNS

In 1991, Joe and Bill sold the studio, including its entire cartoon library, to Turner Broadcasting, which was then planning to launch Cartoon Network and use the Hanna-Barbera library for its programming. Turner paid a whopping $320 million. The deal ran for 20 years with Bill and Joe staying on as advisers. In their new capacities, besides serving on the network's advisory board, they worked collectively and individually on projects of interest under the Hanna-Barbera banner. They executive produced many new shows for first-run syndication, Saturday-morning, and cable network television, including *Bill and Ted's Excellent Adventures*, a spin-off of the hit comedy film series; *Yo Yogi!*, a hipper teenage version of Yogi Bear and other popular Hanna-Barbera characters with some episodes in 3-D; *The Pirates of Dark Water*; *2 Stupid Dogs*; and many others.

In 1993, after being inducted into the Television Academy Hall of Fame, Joe worked separately as an executive producer of the 20th Century Fox feature *Once Upon a Forest* (1993). During the next two years, Bill and he also created several top-rated, made-for-television, feature-length cartoon specials: *I Yabba Dabba Do!*, *Jonny's Golden Quest*, *Hollyrock-a-Bye Baby*, *A Flintstone's Christmas Carol*, and *Jonny Quest vs. the Cyber Insects*.

In 1994, three colossal events occurred in Joe's life. The first was tragic. On January 17, at 4:31 A.M. a magnitude 6.7 earthquake—known as the Northridge earthquake—rocked the ground in the neighboring Los Angeles area, knocking out power and blackening the city. The powerful trembler left massive destruction in its wake, including the destruction of Joe's family's hilltop Sherman Oaks home and furnishings—26 years worth of memories. Emerging physically unscathed, Joe and his wife agreed to rebuild. Three months later, with the earthquake destruction still fresh in his memory, he and Bill witnessed the release of their long-awaited, live-action feature version of *The Flintstones*. Opening on Memorial Day weekend 1994, the 91-minute Universal Pictures comedy, starring John Goodman as Fred Flintstone and Rick Moranis as Barney Rubble, was a huge success, topping more than $130 million domestically and more than $340 million worldwide. As the big-screen version splashed onto movie screens, Joe put his remarkable life story into words, with the publication of his book, *My Life in 'toons: From Flatbush to Bedrock in Under a Century* (Turner Publishing). A year later, Bill cowrote with Tom Ito his own book, *A Cast of Friends*. He also created two original cartoon shorts for Cartoon Network, *Hard Luck Duck* and *Wind-Up Wolf*, his first solo directing efforts since 1941.

Rounding out the decade, Bill and Joe enjoyed renewed success with two storied franchises—The Flintstones and Scooby-Doo.

Joe (left) and Bill flank the author at a May 1993 event honoring the three of them and their fellow Cartoon Network advisory board members. *(Photo by Brian Maurer.) © Jeff Lenburg Collection.*

In 1996, they produced a short-lived spin-off of *The Flintstones* for Cartoon Network, *Cave Kids*, featuring Pebbles and Bamm-Bamm as preschoolers, and a live-action sequel, *The Flintstones: Viva Rock Vegas* (2000). In the interim, they executive produced new direct-to-video adventures: *Scooby-Doo on Zombie Island* (1998), *Scooby-Doo and the Witch's Ghost* (1999), *Scooby-Doo and the Alien Invaders* (2000), and *Scooby-Doo and the Cyber Chase* (2001). They were also executive producers for the first live-action/animated film based on the Scooby-Doo characters, *Scooby-Doo* (2002). The film was a box-office hit for Universal Pictures.

Throughout his life, Bill remained a determined family man who loved his wife and children and supported the philanthropic interests of many charitable organizations, including the Boys Scouts of America, with whom he was a charter member since his youth. He considered himself blessed in every aspect of his life and remained thoughtful and considerate of others in spite of his enormous success. Despite his failing health in his final months, he remained creatively active writing poetry and music. Then, on March 22, 2001, he died of natural causes in his North Hollywood home. He was 90.

Following the loss of his longtime partner, Joe, a determined survivor at 91, never ceased to pursue new opportunities. He continued going to work every day, saying, "I don't know that I love to work but I love to have new ideas." He was driven to his office in his Mercedes by his assistant, Carlton Clay. Joe had as many as a half-dozen projects in storyboard form, occasionally drawing and painting in his spare time. Back to making more cat-and-mouse adventures, he produced the first *Tom and Jerry* cartoon in 34 years, *Tom and Jerry: The Mansion Cat*. Debuting on April 8, 2001, exclusively on Boomerang, Cartoon Network's sister channel, the seven-minute short, codirected by Karl Toerge, contains much of the old mayhem of the classic *Tom and Jerry* cartoons. Things go haywire in a large, fancy house when Tom's owner (voiced by Barbera) is away and a wild chase ensues after Tom finds Jerry enjoying a mid-morning snack. The two destroy the place in the process. It was the last *Tom and Jerry* cartoon produced by Bill before his death, and by Hanna-Barbera Productions, which was closed and became part of Warner Bros. Animation.

Following the corporate changeover, a man steeped in tradition, Joe, who regretted the passing of their famed studio, commented, "In those days, our cartoon was like a club, people worked there for 25 years. Now when you finish a job they let you go. . . . There are too many conferences nowadays, six people trying to settle on an idea."

Regarding television's changing styles of animation, from audience favorites *The Simpsons* to *South Park*, he said, "Their material for 'The

Simpsons' is good. I salute them. 'South Park'? It seems that everyone who doesn't know how to draw has a TV series."

Whether retreating to his comfortable, rebuilt Sherman Oaks home or Palm Springs estate, Joe still enjoyed the social scene and occasionally kicked up his heels. One of his favorite pastimes was taking part in karaoke, including doing a bit as an *amore* singing Dean Martin.

Beginning in 2002, Joe was involved as an executive producer and guiding force behind the creation of a flurry of productions—a new *Scooby-Doo* series for Kids' WB! and Cartoon Network, *What's New, Scooby-Doo?*; a new half-hour television special, *A Scooby-Doo! Christmas* (2004); the sequel to 2002's smash-hit, live-action/animated feature, *Scooby-Doo 2: Monsters Unleashed* (2004); four new direct-to-video Scooby-Doo productions; and his second new television series in four years, *Shaggy & Scooby-Doo: Get a Clue!* (2006). Likewise, remaining creative as long as he was physically able, he produced five more direct-to-video *Tom and Jerry* films as well.

In March 2005, the Academy of Television Arts & Sciences and Warner Bros. Animation dedicated a wall sculpture in Joe and Bill's honor at the Television Academy's Hall of Fame Plaza in North Hollywood. Joe, Bill's widow Violet, and Joe's daughter Jayne were on hand for its unveiling. At age 94, Joe codirected, coproduced, and wrote a second brand-new Tom and Jerry theatrical short, *The Karateguard*, which opened nationally in theaters in late September. In addition, he executive produced (and received story credit for some of the stories) yet another new cat-and-mouse series for The CW network, *Tom and Jerry Tales*.

On December 18, 2006, living more than four years beyond his partner, Joe, at the age of 95, died of natural causes. His passing marked an end to a breed of animators the likes of which shall never be seen again.

For the award-winning sultans of Saturday morning, their lifetime of achievement and the memories they created shall live on. As Bill once said, "I get the biggest thrill when I hear about the joy and fun that we've given everyone who grew up on our cartoons." Their prodigious volume of work, like their menagerie of famous characters, will endure as living proof of their pioneering spirit, their artistic ingenuity and creativity, and their diversity of styles and methods. While coming up with new concepts and setting new standards for others to follow, with one purpose—to create laughter and entertain audiences of every age—they built an empire of popular entertainment.

SELECTED RESOURCES

For further study of Bill Hanna's and Joe Barbera's career and work, the following resources are recommended.

Filmographies

WILLIAM HANNA

http://www.imdb.com/name/nm0360253/
Complete Web listing of every film and television production from William Hanna's career.

JOSEPH BARBERA

http://www.imdb.com/name/nm0053484/
This detailed filmography covers Joe Barbera's career as a producer, director, actor, writer, and more.

DVD and Home Video Collections

The Flintstones—The Complete First Season (Turner Home Entertainment, 2005)

Four-disc set covering the entire first season, including all 28 original episodes, a chronicle of the series, early television commercials, network promos, trailers, and the lost pilot episode, *The Flagstones.*

Hey There, It's Yogi Bear (Warner Home Video, 2008)

Remastered version of Hanna-Barbera's first animated theatrical feature starring the bungling bear and his cub bear companion from the early

1960's hit syndicated series, featuring several songs including James Darren's rendition of "Ven-e, Ven-o, Ven-a."

The Huckleberry Hound Show, Vol. 1 (Turner Home Entertainment, 2005)

Double-sided disc collection featuring 26 episodes of the laconic, blue hound dog, including never-before-seen color and black-and-white bumpers and bridges, the original pilot with segments in color, and a documentary extra on legendary voice artist Daws Butler.

The Jetsons—The Complete First Season (Turner Home Entertainment, 2004)

Collection of all 24 original first-season episodes, remastered, with commentary on two by Janet Waldo, the voice of Judy Jetson, along with a number of DVD extras, including three brand-new featurettes examining the series: *The Jetsons: The Family of the Future, Space Age Gadgets*, and *Rosey the Robotic Maid*.

The Man Called Flintstone (Turner Home Entertainment, 2004)

Original full-length feature based on the long-running, prime-time ABC sitcom and most successful nighttime cartoon series of its time.

Scooby Doo, Where Are You!—The Complete First and Second Seasons (Turner Home Entertainment, 2004)

Offers 25 vintage episodes, including the premiere episode, *What a Night for a Knight*, on four discs, along with several DVD extras, from this popular late-1960's Saturday morning whodunit series featuring the canine hero and his teenage detective friends.

Tom and Jerry—Spotlight Collection (Warner Home Video, 2004)

This two-disc set includes 40 restored and remastered shorts of Hanna-Barbera's world-famous cat-and-mouse team, beginning with 1943's Oscar-nominated *Yankee Doodle Mouse* and ending with 1956's wide-screen CinemaScope short *Blue Cat Blues*. It also features excerpts of Jerry dancing with Gene Kelly from the musical *Anchors Aweigh* (1945),

Tom and Jerry swimming with Esther Williams in *Dangerous When Wet* (1953), and two behind-the-scenes documentaries.

The Yogi Bear Show—The Complete Series (Turner Home Entertainment, 2005)

Two-disc set offering the original pilot and 33 episodes of this first-run syndicated series, along with a gallery tour of never-before-seen sketches and artwork.

SELECTED BIBLIOGRAPHY

Adams, T. R. *Tom and Jerry: Fifty Years of Cat and Mouse*. New York: Crescent Books, 1991.

Associated Press. "A Cartoon King Is Dead at 90," *Newsday*. Available online. URL: http://www.newsday.com/features/ny-hanna obit,0,282729.story. Posted March 23, 2001.

Associated Press. "Cartoon Creator Joe Barbera Dies," *Dallas Morning News*. Available online. URL: http://www.dallasnews.com/shared-content/dws/ent/stories/121906dnentbarberaobit.1e1b331.html. Posted December 18, 2006.

Barbera, Joseph. *My Life in 'toons: From Flatbush to Bedrock in Under a Century*. Atlanta, Ga.: Turner Publishing, 1994.

BBC News. "The Cartoon Dream Team," *BBC News*. Available online. URL: http://news.bbc.co.uk/2/hi/entertainment/1237649.stm. Posted March 23, 2001.

"Biography for Joseph Barbera," Turner Classic Movies. 2009. Available online. URL: http://www.tcm.com/tcmdb/participant. jsp?spid=9574&apid=89197. Accessed October 12, 2009.

Canemaker, John. "Last Cartoon Emperor of the Golden Age." *Wall Street Journal*. December 21, 2006.

English, Merle. "BROOKLYN DIARY Portrait of the Cartoon Artist As a Young Man," *Newsday*. Available online. URL: http://pqasb. pqarchiver.com/newsday/access/102676617.html?dids=10267661 7:102676617&FMT=ABS&FMTS=ABS:FT&type=current&date=Sep+ 22%2C+1991&author=Merle+English&pub=Newsday+(Combined+

editions)&desc=BROOKLYN+DIARY+Portrait+of+The+Cartoon+Artist+As+a+Young+Man&pqatl=google. Posted September 22, 1991.

Gifford, Denis. "William Hanna: Master Animator Whose Cartoon Creations Included Tom and Jerry and the Flintstones," *The Guardian*. Available online. URL: http://www.guardian.co.uk/news/2001/mar/24/guardianobituaries.filmnews1. Posted March 24, 2001.

Grant, John. *Masters of Animation*. New York: Watson-Guptill Publications, 1994.

Hanna, William, and Tom Ito. *A Cast of Friends*. New York: Da Capo Press, 2000.

International Directory of Company Histories, Vol. 23. Farmington Hills, Mich.: St. James Press, 1998.

Lenburg, Jeff. *The Encyclopedia of Animated Cartoons*, Third Edition. New York: Facts On File, 2009.

Lenburg, Jeff. *The Great Cartoon Directors*. Jefferson, N.C.: McFarland & Co., 1983.

Mullen, Megan. "Hanna, William, and Joseph Barbera: U.S. Television Animators," The Museum of Broadcast Communications. Available online. URL:http://www.museum.tv/archives/etv/H/htmlH/hannawillia/hannawillia.htm. Accessed October 15, 2010.

Savage, Mark. "Hanna Barbera's Golden Age of Animation," *BBC News*. Available online. URL: http://news.bbc.co.uk/2/hi/entertainment/6193603.stm. Posted December 19, 2006.

Sennett, Ted. *The Art of Hanna-Barbera: Fifty Years of Creativity*. New York: Viking Studio Books, 1989.

"Tom and Jerry: Episode Guide," Cartoon Network. Available online. URL: http://www.cartoonnetwork.com/tv_shows/tomjerry/index.html. Accessed October 15, 2010.

Woolery, George W. *Children's Television: The First Thirty-Five Years, 1946–1981: Part 1: Animated Cartoon Series*. Metuchen, N.J.: Scarecrow Press, 1983.

INDEX

Page numbers in *italics* indicate photos or illustrations.

Abbott & Costello 113
Abie the Agent 36
Academy Award nominations 45, 48, 52–54, 69–70
Academy Awards
  awarding of to Quimby 54, *55*
  record number of 11
  for *Tom and Jerry* cartoons 52–55, *53*, 58, *61*, 62–64, *63*, 68
Adams, Lee 109
The Adventures of Gulliver 115
The Adventures of Jonny Quest 106, 128
Adventures of Pow Wow 77
advertising 73–74, 96
Afterschool Specials 121, 125
Alice in Wonderland or What's a Nice Kid Like You Doing in a Place Like This? 108–109
Allen, Bob 33–34
Amazing Chan & the Chan Clan 120
Ambro, Hal 133
American School of Dramatic Art 24
An American Tail 143
Anchors Aweigh 58
animated illustration 106–107

Annie Awards *126*
Arabian Knights 115
The Art of Hanna-Barbera (book) 144
Art Students League 28
Atkinson, G.D. 13
The Atom Ant/Secret Squirrel Show 110
Auggie Doggie and Doggie Daddie 88–89
Avery, Tex 48, 57, 70

Balm Creek Dam 12
The Banana Splits Adventure Hour 115, 117
banking 26, 29
Barbera, Dorothy
  children and 35, 51, 71
  divorce from 105
  as girlfriend 26
  marriage to 30
  separation from 31
Barbera, Jayne 51, 71, 76
Barbera, Jim 21–22
Barbera, Lynn 51, 71
Barbera, Neal Francis 51, 71
Barbera, Sheila 105
Barbera, Tess 23
Barbera, Vincent 21–22
Barge, Ed 49, 54, *55*, 78

159

Bates, Stephanie 23
Benadaret, Bea 95
Benedict, Ed 78, 93–94
The Best of Huck and Yogi 100
Betty Boop and *Popeye* cartoons 29
Bible stories 137–138, *139*
Bickenbach, Richard 49, 54, *55*, 78
Bill and Ted's Excellent Adventures 148
Birdman and the Galaxy Trio 113
The Blackstones 113
Blair, Preston 133
Blanc, Mel 95, 100, 103, 144
blockbooking 64
Blue, Ben 114
Blue Monday 34
Bogle, Jack 29
The Book of Knowledge 24
Bosko series 17
Bosley, Tom 120
Bowsky, William 29
boxing 25
Boy Scouts 13
Bradley, Scott 50
Bray, J.R. 37
Broadway Medley of 1936 50
Broadway shows 24
Brooklyn Academy of Music 24
Brun-Cottan, Francoise 65
Busy Buddies 70
Butler, Daws 79, 92, 95, 100, 144

C

Caldwell, Mo 19
Calvacca, Francesca 21
Captain and the Kids 33–38
caricatures *104, 119*
Carr, John 44
Cartoon Network 147
Cassidy, Ted 114
Cast of Friends (Hanna and Ito) 148
The Cat Concerto 61, *62*
The Cattanooga Cats 117
Cave Kids 149

Challenge of the GoBots 140
Chaplin, Charlie 14
Charlotte's Web 121–124, *123*
C.H.O.M.P.S. 127
CinemaScope 68
Cohn, Harry 77–78
college of animation 126–127
Collier's 28
color 79
Columbia Pictures 91
comic-book superheroes 124
commercials 73–74, 96
Compton High School 15
computer-generated imagery (CGI)
    animation 143
Connal, Scott 124
*A Connecticut Yankee in King Arthur's
    Court* 24
Conried, Hans 68
Corden, Henry 130
costumes 86
Count Screwloose 37
Crusader Rabbit 76, 81
Cubby Bear 30
Curtin, Hoyt 82–83
Cyrano 121

D

Danger Island 115
Dangerous When Wet 66, *67*
*Dastardly & Muttley in Their Flying
    Machines* 115, *116*
Davis, Manny 30
death of Bill Hanna 150
death of Joe Barbera 151
Deitch, Gene 72
Denby, T.B.S 12
Dirks, Rudolf 33
Disney, Walt 18, 28
 Dr. Jekyll and Mr. Mouse 62
Downs, Charlie 133
The Dutchman (school newspaper) 24
Dynomutt, Dog Wonder 126

E

Earl, Dorothy. *See* Barbera, Dorothy
earthquakes 148
Emmy Awards
for *ABC Afterschool Specials* 121, 125
for *The Flintstones* 98, 109
for *The Huckleberry Hound Show* 89
for *Jack and the Beanstalk* 114
for *The Smurfs* cartoons 133
Erasmus Hall High School 21, 23–25

F

Fairbanks, Douglas 14
Fantastic Four 113
Farmer Al Falfa 30
Father Was a Robot 106
Felix the Cat comics 14, 29
Fleischer Studios 29
The Flintstones cartoons
birth of Pebbles and 105
decline of 109
development of 93–98, *95, 98*
The Flintstone Comedy Hour 120
in foreign markets 106
live-action movies 148, 149
The Man Called Flintstone 111–113, *112*
The New Fred and Barney Show 129, 130
Pebbles & Bamm-Bamm 119
reruns of on Saturday mornings 117
theme song for 82
Foray, June 95
Foster, Warren 82, 91, 97
Freleng, Isadore "Friz" 33, 36, 43, 62
Froelich, Arthur 104
The Funtastic World of Hanna-Barbera 137

G

Gallopin' Gals 43, 44
The Gathering 127
Gerald McBoing-Boing 65
Gillett, Burt 30
Give and Tyke 71
GoBots: War of the Rock Lords 140
Golden Eagle Award 138
Golden Globe Awards 98
Goodman, John 148
Good Will to Men 69–70
The Goose Goes South 44
Gordon, Dan 30, 31, 33, 82, 93–94
Gordon, George 33
Grape Ape 125
Grauman's Chinese Theater 134
Great Depression 15
The Greatest Adventure: Stories from the Bible 137–138, *139*
Gross, Milt 37
The Gruesomes 102

H

Hagar the Horrible 143
Halas, George 86
Hamilton, Irene 18
Hanna, Avice Joyce 12, 14
Hanna, Bonnie 38, 54
Hanna, David 38, 54
Hanna, Norma 14
Hanna, Violet 19, 51
Hanna, William John 12–15
The Hanna-Barbera New Cartoon Series 103
Hanna-Barbera Productions 73–76, *75,* 89–91
Hanna-Barbera's Superstars 10 141
Hardcase 121
Hard Luck Duck 148
The Harlem Globetrotters 119
Harman, Hugh 16, 37, 38
Harman-Ising Studios 16–20
Hawkins, Emery 33

Hazelton, Gene 74
Heidi's Song 133–134, *135*
The Herculoids 113
Hershfield, Harry 36
Hey There, It's Yogi Bear 106, *107*
Hickman, Dwayne 114
hockey 124–125
Holden, Sheila. *See* Barbera, Sheila
Holiday in Mexico 60
Hollywood Walk of Fame star 126
Holy Innocents school 23
The Honeymooners 93
The Huckleberry Hound Show 78, 82–88, *83, 87, 89*
Hughes, Howard 66
Hungarian Rhapsody No. 2 62
Hunt, Gordon 67

I

I Love Lucy 74
Invitation to Dance 65–66
Irving Trust Bank 26, 29
Ising, Rudolf 16, 17–18, 37, 38, 42, 45, 52. *See also* Harman-Ising Studios
Iwerks, Ub 28

J

Jack and the Beanstalk 114
Jasper and Jinx 39–44. *See also Tom and Jerry* cartoons
The Jetsons 82, 102, 103–104, 111, 128, 137
The Jetsons: The Movie 143–144, *145*
Jitterbug Follies 37
Johann Mouse 68
Jokebook 136
jokes 51
Jones, Chuck 72, 128
Jonny Quest 106, *108, 109*
Josie & the Pussycats 119

K

The Karateguard 151
Katz, Ray 16
The Katzenjammer Kids 33
Keavy, Hubbard 42–43
Kellogg's 83, 96, 103
Kelly, Gene 58–60, *59,* 65–66, 114
Kelly, Ray 30, 31, 33
Kiko the Kangaroo 30
King Leonardo and His Short Subjects 81
Kirschner, David 143
Kling Studios 73

L

Lah, Michael 57, 70, 78
Lamas, Fernando 66
The Last of the Curlews 121
Laurel & Hardy 111
layoffs 72
licensing 89, 96, 99–100, *100,* 125
limited animation 78–79
Lippy the Lion 103
Liszt, Franz 62
The Little Orphan 62–64
live-action films 120–121, 127, 148
Looney Tunes 18, 33
Loopy de Loop 91
Love, Harry 127
Love American Style 120
Love and the Old-Fashioned Father 120
Love That Pup 71

M

Magic Land of Allakazam 100
The Magilla Gorilla Show 106, 111
The Maid and the Martian 66–67
Maltese, Michael 82, 89, 91
Mamma's New Hat 38
Mannix, Eddie 54, *55,* 72
Marcel wave 21
Marshall, Lewis 70, 78
mascots 124–125

*M*A*S*H* 68
Mayer, Louis B. 60
Meet Me in St. Louis 50
merchandise, licensed 89, 96, 99–100, *100*, 125
Merrie Melodies 18, 33
Messick, Don 79, 92, 144
Metro-Goldwyn-Mayer (MGM) 19–20, 30–31
Meyers, Mike 31
Micro Ventures 115
The Midnight Snack 47–48
The Milky Waif 60
The Milky Way 52
Mitchell, John H. 76–78, 83, 93
Moby Dick and the Mighty Mightor 113
Moranis, Rick 148
Motormouse & Autocat 117
Mouse Trouble 58
Movieola projectors 17
Muir, Roger 78
Murrow, Edward R. 85
Muse, Kenneth 49, 54, *55*, 78
music 18, 82–83
My Life in 'toons (Barbera) 148

N

Nessie Come Home 134
The New Adventures of Huck Finn 115–116
The New Fred and Barney Show 129, 130
The New Yogi Bear Show 143
Nichols, Charles A. 133
The Night Before Christmas 48
Nixon, Marni 114
novelty merchandise 89, 96, 99–100, *100*, 125

O

Officer Pooch 44
Ogden, Jack 13
O'Hanlon, George 103, 144
Old Rockin' Chair Tom 27
One Droopy Knight 70
Oscars. *See* Academy Awards

P

Pacific Title & Art Studio 16
Pantages Theatre 15
Pat and Mike 74
Patterson, Ray 49
Peck, C.L. 15
Pepe 96
Perez, Bill 134
The Perils of Penelope Pitstop 115, 116, 117
Peter Potamus and His Magic Flying Balloon 106
Peter Puck 124–125
Petunia National Park 37
Phool Phan Phables 37
Pickford, Mary 14
Pirate Jack 134
Pixie and Dixie cartoons 82, 83
plagiarism 62
planned animation 78–79
Popeye 29
pranks 51
Pratt Institute 28–29
Preminger, Ingo 68
Puss Gets the Boot 41–43, 45

Q

The Quick Draw McGraw Show 88–91, *90*
Quiet Please! 58
Quimby, Fred
  Academy Awards and 54, *55*
  advertising and 74
  Gene Kelly and 59–60
  hiring of Bill Hanna by 20
  hiring of Joe Barbera by 31
  image of *27*
  Joe Barbera's play and 67

MGM's new cartoon studio and 32–37

retirement of 70

teaming of Hanna and Barbera and 38

Tom and Jerry cartoons and 40–41, 43, 45

R

racial stereotypes 57
Rah Rah Bear 86
Rainbow Parades 30
Randolph, Lillian 47
Redbook 28
Reed, Alan 95–96, 130
Rhapsody in Rivets 62
Riha, Bobby 114
Robin Hoodwinked 66
Rock Odyssey 134–136
The Roman Holidays 120
Rotoscoping 60
Royal Cat Nap 68
Ruby, Joe 118
Ruff and Reddy 76–77
The Ruff and Reddy Show 79–81, 80, 85
The Runaways 125

S

Samson & Goliath 113
Saturday Evening Post 28
Scaramouche 74
Schallert, Edwin 65
Schell, Ronnie 124
Schlesinger, Leon 16, 18, 36
Scooby-Doo cartoons
    direct-to-video adventures 149
    later series 151
    live action movie 150
    Scooby-Doo and Scrappy-Doo 128, 130
    Scooby-Doo, Where Are You! 116, 116, 117–118

Screen Gems 76–78, 86, 91
Sealab 2020 120
Seal Skinners 37
Shazzan 113
Short, Besa 45
Shows, Charles 82
Sidney, George 58, 60, 73, 96
Sidney, I.K. 74
Silverman, Fred 110, 117–118, 128, 131
"Sing Before Breakfast" 50
Singer, Al 25
Sinkin' in the Bathtub 17
Skeleton Dance 28
Smith, Cecil 85
Smith, Hal 100
The Smurfs 131–133, *132*
Snagglepuss 100
Snoper and Blabber 88
Sommer, Paul 33
songs 18, 82–83
Southworth, Ken 70
Space Ghost and Dino Boy 111
The Space Kidettes 111
Sparks, Bea 66
Spears, Ken 119
Spence, Irven 15, 49, 54, *55*, 133
Spielberg, Stephen 143
Spike and Tyke 71
Stanton, Frank 118
Stevens, Jack 16
Strouse, Charles 109
Swing Social 44

T

Taft Broadcasting Company 113, 127
Takamoto, Iwao 118
Taylor, Robert 133–134
Technicolor 64
television 60, 72, 73–76, 79–80, 136
Terry, Paul 30

TerryToons Studio 30–31
That's My Pup 71
theme parks 143
theme songs 82–83
The Three Musketeers 115
Tiffany 144
Toerge, Karl 150
Tom and Chérie 68
Tom and Jerry cartoons
 attempts to revive 72
 Busy Buddies 70
 The Cat Concerto 61, 62
 changing appearance in 57
 development of 39–44
 Dr. Jekyll and Mr. Mouse 62
 Hatch Up Your Troubles 64
 Jerry's Cousin 64–65
 Johann Mouse 68
 The Karateguard 151
 The Little Orphan 62–64
 Love That Pup 71
 The Midnight Snack 47–48
 The Milky Waif 60
 Mouse Trouble 58
 naming of characters in *39*, 44
 The Night Before Christmas 48
 Old Rockin' Chair Tom 27
 production of 48–51
 Puss Gets the Boot 41–43, 45
 Quiet Please! 58
 Robin Hoodwinked 66
 Royal Cat Nap 68, 70
 That's My Pup 71
 Tom and Chérie 68
 Tom and Jerry Kids 146
 The Tom & Jerry Show 125
 Tom and Jerry Tales 151
 Tom and Jerry: The Mansion Cat 150
 Tom and Jerry: The Movie 146–147
 Tot Watchers 70, 72
 Touché, Pussy Cat! 68
 Two Little Indians 69
 The Two Mouseketeers 62, 63, 65
 Yankee Doodle Mouse 52, 53

Top Cat 100, 102, 104, 111
To Spring 19, 20
Tot Watchers 70, 72
Touché, Pussy Cat! 68
Touché Turtle 103
"The Trolley Song" 50
Turner Broadcasting 146–147
Tweedy, Bill 13
Tweety Pie 62
The Two Faces of Janus 66
Two Little Indians 69
The Two Mouseketeers 62, 63, 65, 68

U

The Ups & Downs of Mr. Phool Phan 37

V

Van Beuren Studios 29–30
Vander Pyl, Jean 95
Vinci, Carlo 78
violence 57, 58, 146

W

The Wacky Races 115
Wait Till Your Father Gets Home 120
Waldo, Janet 114
Walker, Mort 94
Wally Gator 103
Wanted: No Master 37
War Dogs 55–57
war-related instructional shorts 55
We'll Take Manhattan 114
What a Lion! 34
What's New, World 114
When Magoo Flew 68
Where's Huddles? 119
Williams, Esther 66, *67*
Wind-Up Wolf 148
Wogatzke, Violet. *See* Hanna, Violet
Wolf Hounded 91

X

Xerography 122

Y

Yakky Doodle 100
Yankee Doodle Mouse 52

Yogi Bear cartoons 82, 86, 87, 99–101, 106, *107*, 143
The Yogi Bear Show 99, *100*

Z

Zander, Jack 30, 31, 33

ABOUT THE AUTHOR

Jeff Lenburg is an award-winning author, celebrity biographer, and nationally acknowledged expert on animated cartoons who has spent nearly three decades researching and writing about this lively art. He has written nearly 30 books—including such acclaimed histories of animation as *Who's Who in Animated Cartoons*, *The Great Cartoon Directors*, and four previous encyclopedias of animated cartoons. His books have been nominated for several awards, including the American Library Association's "Best Non-Fiction Award" and the Evangelical Christian Publishers Association's Gold Medallion Award for "Best Autobiography/ Biography." He lives in Arizona.

Photo courtesy: Brian Maurer.